In

B62A

B62A        9:45 AM       MEXICO CITY

# In & Out of Place

Library of Congress Cataloging-in-Publication Data

Names: Civil, Gabrielle, author.
Title: In and out of place : Mexico/performance/writing / Gabrielle Civil.
Other titles: In & out of place | Innovative prose.
Description: First edition. | Huntsville, Texas : TRP:The University Press
   of SHSU, [2022] | Series: Innovative prose | Includes index.
Identifiers: LCCN 2022010679 (print) | LCCN 2022010680 (ebook) | ISBN
   9781680032796 (paperback) | ISBN 9781680032802 (ebook)
Subjects: LCSH: Civil, Gabrielle—Travel—Mexico. | Civil,
   Gabrielle—Diaries. | African American women performance
   artists—Mexico. | Performance art—Mexico. | Identity (Philosophical
   concept) in art. | Feminism in art. | Mexico—Description and travel. |
   LCGFT: Autobiographies. | Creative nonfiction. | Artists' books.
Classification: LCC NX512.C57 A2 2022b  (print) | LCC NX512.C57  (ebook) |
   DDC 709.2—dc23/eng/20220722
LC record available at https://lccn.loc.gov/2022010679
LC ebook record available at https://lccn.loc.gov/2022010680

FIRST EDITION

Front cover image courtesy: Camilo Hannibal Smith

Cover design by PJ Carlilse

Printed and bound in the United States of America
First Edition Copyright: 2024

TRP: The University Press of SHSU
Huntsville, Texas 77341

texasreviewpress.org

# In & Out of Place

Mexico / performance / writing

## Gabrielle Civil

**Innovative Prose**

TRP: The University Press of SHSU

Huntsville, Texas 77341

"¿Estamos aquí para comunicarnos? ¿Estamos aquí para el intercambio cultural?
Entonces no seamos estrechos de miras. No seamos pequeños y egoístas . . .
La comunicación debe significar intercambio."

"Are we here to communicate? Are we here for cultural interchange?
Then let us not be narrow. Let us not be small and selfish . . .
Communication should mean interchange."

—Elizabeth Catlett Mora

# In & Out of Place

"Como mis temas han sido siempre mis sensaciones, mis estados de ánimo y las reacciones profundas que la vida ha producido en mí, yo lo he llevado objetivamente y plasmado en las figuras que hago de mí misma, que es lo más sincero y real que he podido hacer para expresar lo que yo he sentido dentro y fuera de mi."

"Since my subjects have always been my sensations, my states of mind and the profound reactions that life has been producing in me, I have frequently objectified all this in figures of myself, which were the most sincere and real thing that I could do in order to express what I felt inside and outside. . ."

—Frida Kahlo

# IN AND OUT OF PLACE

Walking down the street in Mexico City, I think of Mexican artist Frida Kahlo's phrase *figures of myself*. *"Morenita,"* a man calls out with a friendly voice. *"Cho-co-la-te,"* another intones, blowing me kisses. Which figures of myself are these men encountering? What is happening "inside and outside?" *Race doesn't matter*, many Mexicans I met would say. *It's you gringos that have that problem*. When I moved through Mexican spaces, however—beaches in Playa del Carmen, carnival in Mérida, churches in Guanajuato, subway rides in the capital—something different was happening. My racial difference was acknowledged and marked in multiple ways; yet, along with my gender, my class, my age, my size, my citizenship and more, this difference functioned differently than in the United States. I was different, both as and to myself.

In Mexico, my race, my body, my preconceptions as a black woman artist, were both in and out of place. My experience of these new and different "sensations, states of mind and . . . profound reactions" stimulated new possibilities for my conceptual and performance art. "In and Out of Place: Making Black Performance Art in Mexico" is the manifestation of these possibilities.

This project first sparked during my sabbatical from St. Catherine University. In mid-January 2007, I came to Mexico to improve my oral Spanish, engage Mexican culture, and work on my hybrid critical-creative text *Swallow the Fish: Adventures in Black Feminist Performance Art*. A part of this last entailed thinking deeply about race, gender and body in my own work.

For the first six weeks, I hung out on the beach, took Spanish classes, wrote and traveled to a few cities before deciding to head to the capital. I arrived in la Cuidad de México, Distrito Federal on a one way ticket, knowing absolutely nobody.

It didn't take long for me to fall in love . . .

Bajando una calle de la Ciudad de México, pienso en la frase de la artista mexicana Frida Kahlo *'figuras que hago de mí misma'*. *'Morenita',* grita un hombre con voz gentil. *'Chocolate',* entona otro, lanzándome besos. ¿Qué figuras de mi ser encuentran estos hombres? ¿Qué está ocurriendo "dentro y fuera"? *La raza no importa,* decían muchos mexicanos que conocí. *Ustedes son, los gringos, los que tienen ese problema.* Sin embargo, cuando me moví por ciertos ambientes mexicanos—la costa de Playa del Carmen, el Carnaval de Mérida, las iglesias de Guanajuato, los trayectos en metro por la capital— sucedía algo distinto. Mi diferencia racial era acusada y se marcaba de múltiples formas; de hecho, además de mi género, mi clase social, mi edad, mi estatura, mi nacionalidad, etc., esta diferencia (la racial) funcionaba de otra manera que en Estados Unidos. Yo era diferente, como yo misma y para mí misma.

En México, mi raza, mi cuerpo, mis ideas preconcebidas como artista negra, se encuadraban por igual dentro y fuera de lugar. La vivencia de estas nuevas y dispares "sensaciones, estados de ánimo y… reacciones profundas" me estimuló posibilidades insólitas para el desarrollo de mi arte performático y conceptual. *"In and Out of Place: Making Black Performance Art in Mexico"* - *"Dentro y Fuera de Lugar: Creando Arte de Acción Afro-Feminista en México"* es la manifestación de estas posibilidades.

Este proyecto generó su primer chispazo durante mi descanso sabático de la Universidad de St. Catherine. A mediados de enero de 2007, fui a México para mejorar mi español hablado, mezclarme con la cultura mexicana, y trabajar en mi texto híbrido crítico-creativo *"Swallow the Fish: Adventures in Black Feminist Performance Art"* (*"Trágate el pez: Aventuras en el Arte de Acción Afro-Feminista"*). Parte de este texto, acabó por alumbrar el pensamiento profundo sobre raza, género y cuerpo que alienta mi propio trabajo.

Durante las primeras seis semanas, pasé tiempo en la playa, tomé clases de español, escribí y viajé a algunas ciudades antes de decidir dirigirme a la capital. Llegué a Ciudad de México, Distrito Federal, con un billete de ida y sin conocer a nadie.

No necesité mucho tiempo para enamorarme . . .

# BÉSAME MUCHO

El metro / The subway.

Crisscrossing the city.

Taxis and el Metrobús.

Insurgents!

A long boulevard of majestic palms.

Paseo de la Reforma.

A coronation.

El Ángel.

On foot.

Desire paths.

Doorbells and letters.

Invitations.

Glorietas.

A welcome/ Un bienvenidos.

\*

It wasn't my first day in Mexico City, but it felt like another beginning.

I was sitting in a park, eating a mini-yogurt, and reading the newspaper. My spirits were high because Casa Tarami, the guest house where I was staying, was cozy and had cable. Gabriel and Katy the hosts were kind and warm. I also liked what I had on. My skirt was pretty and twirly and made me feel good. The sun was shining in winter and I wasn't in Minnesota living my usual life.

"Con permiso, do you know where I can find tal y tal address?" a voice above me said.

A tall, handsome young man had appeared out of thin air. He had seen me before I even saw him. He had short dark hair, round cheeks, and piercing eyes. This dreamboat was asking me for directions? Much later, I asked if his question had been a ploy. Clearly, I wasn't from there. But C. always claimed that he was sincere. He said that many foreigners lived in that part of the city, Cuauhtémoc, not far from the U.S. embassy, and so he thought it possible that I would know.

"Lo siento, no sé. I'm actually looking for places myself. I'm curious about rents."

"Well, I saw some Se Renta signs right around here. Would you like me to show you?"

Who was this black girl throwing her yogurt cup away, folding up her newspaper, and following a man she didn't even know to go learn about empty apartments? My homegirls in Detroit would shake their heads. But something about him seemed good, trustworthy. He took me to see the For Rent signs and we jotted down the contact numbers. As it turned out, he was a messenger delivering invitations to an art opening. I joined him on his route and went to art galleries and museums all around the city. He would ring the bell and I would catch a glimpse of paintings, sculptures, marionettes, artifacts, curators, secretaries, doormen, and artists.

We strolled the boulevards, ringing doorbells, chatting and getting to know each other. He was both serious and easy with a low-grade crackle of sexual energy. We took the Metrobús and the subway, where he precisely and deliberately gave me back my change. In one taxi, "Bésame Mucho" came on and the driver turned it up. We all sang along, and I looked out the window and saw palm trees, El Ángel with her crown, shimmering with magic.

# MINERVA CAVES

In Playa del Carmen, a painted man in generic finery traded photo ops for cash. Wandering mariachis dressed all in white played guitars on the sand. For four straight nights in Mérida, beer company goddesses rode loud, bright carnival floats. These goddesses danced, waved, and projectile threw snack bags to (or sometimes at) the crowd. I'd seen love birds in embraces, arguments in cars, complicated public transactions, and I was enthralled by it all. Still, I was craving performance art in Mexico. Something deliberately, self-consciously artsy, this thing that I claimed as my craft. Here in Mexico City, at the Tamayo Museum, Doa Aly's videos showed the Egyptian artist taking ballet lessons, fumbling, and striving. Yes, something like that, but I wanted it live. The museum exhibition was called *Snap Judgments*. I followed its advice.

On my way to Spanish class, crossing Paseo de la Reforma, I had to pass El Ángel. Long, shallow, sandy steps led to dark statues, a lion in laurels leading a child, and higher up, more sand-blasted white figures. They all looked like men. There was so much history and mythology that I didn't know, but I would cross the street and look each day and try to figure it out. Many insurgents were laid to rest there and many heroes of independence. At the very top on a tall column, stood the angel herself, shining brightly, covered with gold. In one hand, she held a wreath, in the other a broken shackle.

That day, though, something was different. Right across from the monument on Florencia Avenue hung a huge banner with an image of that gilded Ángel now holding a black flag. Almost imperceptible on the flag was the word "Digna" or "Worthy." The banner said: "Monumenta: el 8 de marzo, el día internacional de la mujer." It said: "Minerva Cuevas." Then in smaller letters, the names: Mónica Mayer, Mónica Castillo, Verena Grimm, Fabiola Torres-Alzaga, Lorena Wolffer, and Maris Bustamente.

¡Mónica Mayer! We had just been reading about Mónica Mayer the day before in my Spanish class. We each had been assigned to bring in an article of our choice, and I had brought "El Arte de Performance en

México" by Josefina Alcázar from her book *Performance y Teatralidad.*" We read: "La performancera mexicana Mónica Mayer, recuerda su experiencia de cuando era estudiante y se enteró de la existencia del arte conceptual: 'se me abrieron las puertas a todas las posibilidades, de un brochazo se eliminaban las fronteras entre lo teórico y lo artístico . . .'"

In my notebook, I translated: "The Mexican performance artist Mónica Mayer recalls her experience as a student when she first became aware of conceptual art: 'it opened up for me the doors of every possibility, in one brush stroke, it eliminated the borders between theory and artistic practice. . ."And with that sentence, I was back in the Art Library at the University of Michigan, looking at images, writing poems, and learning about conceptual art myself. I don't draw or paint and felt so grateful that there could be other ways to be an artist. It thrilled me to think of Mónica Mayer as a young Mexican woman artist having these same feelings. It thrilled me even more the coincidence of just having had her words in my head, in my notebook, and then seeing this poster with her name in Mexico City the next day.

"Discúlpame, Señor," I said to the tourist police officer. And in a quick, Spanish jumble, I got out "el día internacional de la mujer," Mónica Mayer, performance, where and when? He told me that something small had happened at El Ángel that morning (Oh no, had I missed it?!) but the real events hadn't started yet. He told me to catch a bus to go to the Zócalo, the central plaza of downtown Mexico City, and that at 10 AM (the exact starting time of my class and exactly 20 minutes from that moment), there would be meetings and performances and marches for International Women's Day. And there I could find Mónica Mayer.

So I made a snap judgment. Against years of sensibility and training as a student and teacher, I skipped class, caught a bus, and headed for the Zócalo. Desperately Seeking Mónica Mayer! When I arrived, of course, the plaza was empty. Had the tourist officer mistaken the time or the day? Maybe I could still catch the celebration? Again stumbling, jumbling at the tourist info kiosk, I tried again: "Mónica Mayer, el día de la mujer, arte de performance, a las diez, etc." After much research, telephone calls, and a stint on the internet, the guapo at the desk opened up a brochure for me and pointed at Museo Ex Teresa Arte Actual. "This place is just around the corner. They'll probably be able to help you."

Five minutes later, I was talking my way into the office of Juan Carlos Jaurena, the director of Ex Teresa who led me to Edith Medina, the curator of the Centro de Documentación. After we introduced ourselves, Edith promptly said to me: "Oh Gabrielle, I think I got your e-mail..." And it was true, a couple weeks before, I had sent an e-mail responding to a call for performance art proposals that I saw in *Tiempo Libre*, a Mexico City arts weekly. I hadn't yet received a response and wasn't sure if my e-mail—or my Spanish—had gone awry. In that moment, I put it together: that call for proposals had come from Ex Teresa and that my wild goose chase for Mónica Mayer was making my dreams come true.

A performance artist herself, Edith was extremely nice, generous, and helpful. She gave me the websites and phone numbers of major women performance artists in Mexico including Lorena Wolffer, Rocío Boliver (aka La Congelada de Uva), and the mismísima Mónica Mayer! Edith talked to me about the Centro de Documentación and the situation of performance art in Mexico. She explained their ongoing review of performance proposals and the opportunity for artists around the world to present work at the museum. "Tell me what you're trying to do and we can help," she said. "Gracias, gracias, gracias." I said. I was blown away...

Housed in an eighteenth-century church, formerly the Convent of St. Teresa, hence the name, Ex Teresa Arte Actual is a contemporary, experimental art museum with the most comprehensive performance art archives in the country. The next day, I'll return with a proper appointment at the Centro de Documentación. I'll spend all day reviewing photographs, videos, and articles about Mexican performance art. I'll call prominent women performance artists on the phone, arranging meetings to talk about art, experience, and the body.

Of course, the first person on my list is Mónica Mayer. And when I meet her, Lorena Wolffer, and Rocío Boliver, I'll thank them and ask them about their work and lives. I'll share with them my own stories of art and imagination and coincidence. I'll tell them how inspired I was by the Monumenta Project to reinterpret major female icons in the city; and later, I'll ask their help to come back to Mexico City and make more art for real. My acquaintance with Edith, Mónica and her husband Victor Lerma, Lorena Wolffer, and La Congelada would extend over many months and change my life.

I never did get a chance to meet Minerva Cuevas. She was out of town during that first trip to Mexico City and it somehow slipped my mind to look her up later. I must confess that when I first saw "Minerva Cuevas" in big letters on the banner, I didn't know that was the Mexican woman artist who produced the image. Only when Edith gave me the list of artists, did I realize her name was there.

Standing that day below El Ángel, I thought "Minerva Cuevas" was the title of a new performance art piece that would happen in Mexico City. In that performance, women would gambol over lions in laurels, children, heroes, and insurgents. Women would climb to the top of a monument and brandish a black flag. Women would make noise, stop traffic, and chance the circulation in the city. All those women on the banner, the Mexican women artists I would meet and the ones I wouldn't, they would all be a part of it. And I would be a part of it too.

We would all be Minerva Cuevas in Mexico City! A hybrid mixture of "Minerva," Roman goddess of wisdom, all white stone, and "Cuevas" or caves, dark indentations, damp impressions, earthy hollows. This performance was already happening in my head. Maybe it would even happen that day! Somehow, I would find these women, run up to them and say "I'm here! I am one of you! I am a Minerva Cueva too!" More than anything, I wanted to make this performance real.

# A HEATED POOL

It's always a risk to reach out to someone you admire.

What if you don't end up drinking smoothies together, swapping holiday cards, or collaborating on a new fashion line? What if your brain freezes and you can't fully get out why you're there or you gush and the other person doesn't give up much, or your questions fall flat or you just seem like a creeper, or worse, a fan, and not a full-blooded artist in your own right. What if your hero (or as my mentor Dr. Toni C. King says, your shero / hero / theyro) turns out to be an asshole? Or you end up coming off as one? As an extrovert, I've had some awkward encounters. I've also had some moments of grace.

On the corner of Bleecker and Christopher Street in Manhattan, right outside the sixth-floor walkup where I lived, bell hooks was standing on the corner. Her afro, parted down the middle, was so large it seemed like arms reaching out toward the sky.

"Ms. hooks," I said hustling out my building door, wanting to catch her before she crossed the street.

"Hello," she turned and smiled.

"Call me Gloria. What's your name?"

"I'm Gabrielle Civil and I'm a poet studying Comp Lit at NYU and my friend Ira is in your class at Brooklyn College."

"Well, you should be in my class too," she said.

My heart filled with joy. I saw her other times later speaking on distinguished panels, but that was the only direct conversation we ever had. And there she was inviting me, literally a black girl on the street, to come and study with her. That was black feminist community.

At NYU, I got a taste of this through Yari Yari, a symposium of Black Women Writers from around the world organized by Jayne Cortez, Cheryll Y. Greene, Crystal Williams, and other members of the Organization of Women Writers of Africa. In 1997, my pal Rosa and I volunteered at the first convening, "Yari Yari: Black Women Writers and the Future." We met Octavia Butler, J. E. Franklin, Louise Meriwether, Rashidah Ismaili, and so many other black feminist icons. A powerhouse of poetry and jazz, Jayne remained a radiant presence in our lives. She shared an especially close relationship with Rosa but was also wonderful to me. In 2006, when Jayne heard that I was heading to Mexico, she offered to share Elizabeth Catlett's contact information. To this day, Catlett is perhaps the most famous expatriate African American woman artist in Mexico. Born in 1915, she pushed back against racist barriers in the art world and used her work to showcase the beauty and dignity of black people.

While she originally studied painting and drawing (including with the trailblazing Lois Mailou Jones), Catlett became best known for her sculptures and prints. She developed her printmaking practice in Taller de Gráfica Popular (People's Graphic Arts Workshop) in Mexico City. She first went to Mexico City in 1946 with her first husband, Charles White. La flecha de amor struck with Mexican artist Francisco Mora, another member of TGP. So after briefly returning to the US to obtain a divorce, she returned to Mexico to live, to love, and to make art imbued with populism and social justice. In 1947, she married Mora (nicknamed Pancho). They raised three sons and remained together until his death in 2002.

In 1959, Catlett also became the first woman professor of sculpture at Escuela Nacional de Artes Plásticas at the Universidad Nacional Autónoma de México (UNAM), one of the top universities in the world. The male faculty at the time protested her hire (too female, too black). Nevertheless, she persisted and ended up mentoring generations of Latin American artists. After her retirement in 1975, Catlett focused full-time on her art and exhibited her work worldwide. In 2005, I received Melanie Anne Herzog's monograph on Catlett for Christmas. And in 2007, when I was traveling in Mexico on sabbatical, Elizabeth Catlett was ninety-two years old, living in Cuernavaca.

*

One of the best things about being in a different country is how perceptions of distance shift. As poor undergrads, my friends and I didn't think twice about riding the train for twelve hours to go from one European country to another. Two decades later, my friend Raewyn from New Zealand would book field trips for our students in Ohio to go by car to Saint Louis. ("Why not? It's not that far," she said.) In the meantime, it used to take a bribe to get native New Yorkers to travel from Brooklyn to the Bronx. And let's not even talk about suburbanites coming into the kingdom of Detroit in my youth. Too far, too black, too dangerous. Anyway, my Spanish language school in Playa del Carmen was nowhere near Cuernavaca. Still, I kept her phone number close and safe. A black feminist pilgrimage awaited.

Even after I left Playa and landed in Mexico City, it took a while to screw up the nerve to call. I didn't have her email address, so I had to buy a local cell phone and Telcel SIM card. I also had to be ready to explain over the phone in my wonky Spanish who I was and why I was calling. Still as Debbie Allen famously announced, "Fame costs. And right here's where you start paying *in sweat*." So I mopped my brow, screwed up my courage, took a deep breath, and called. The great lady answered the phone herself.

"Who are you? Jayne gave you my contact?"

She paused for a moment after my spiel.

"Well, why don't you come over for lunch.

Bring your bathing suit. We have a heated pool."

I took the bus from Mexico City to Cuernavaca, about forty-five minutes away, bearing flowers and butterflies in my stomach. It was happening! The house was impressive, full of books and artworks and family photos. It had that well-worn family feeling. Señora Catlett herself was light-skinned, cacahuete colored, with white hair. She seemed a little frail, moved slowly, but her wit was quick. She was remarkably easy going and fun. We chatted about Mexican buses and art, how much Mexico City had changed. I asked her if she knew Frida Kahlo and she laughed.

"I didn't know her well, but we were at some of the same meetings. That woman was so poor! She suffered so much in her lifetime and, back then, so many people wouldn't give her the time of day. It's amazing how they talk about her now. Frida would laugh so hard."

Señora Catlett's eyes twinkled. I loved the chisme, but time had been flying. I started to gather my things to head out the door.

"Where are you going?" she asked.

"Oh, I just noticed the time. I need to catch the bus back."

"Why don't you just stay the night here? It would be a lot easier."

"Well, I don't want to be a bother," I said.

12

"You only mentioned the afternoon."

"Well, I didn't know who you were before.

Now, I know you. Stay a while."

And so I changed into my suit and slid into divine, warm waters.

*

Was that when I knew for sure I'd live in Mexico?

*

I only got to see Señora Catlett one more time before she died. She allowed me to visit her on my thirty-fifth birthday. I brought more flowers, sweets, and a copy of my *Elizabeth Catlett* book for her to sign. Her son David welcomed me kindly. He was worried about his mother's health. Upstairs resting in bed, she seemed a little more frail, but she still had that sparkle in her eye. I pulled up a chair for more chisme.

"Qué tal Señora Catlett?" I said with a smile. "Today is my birthday!"

"¡Feliz Cumpleaños!"

She showed me drawings for a Mahalia Jackson memorial she was designing and advised me to always keep up my mind. "Even if your body goes, if you keep working on things, you'll be okay." Then she mentioned something about Oprah's Legends Ball, and I was like, "Wait, you were at Oprah's Legends Ball?" And she was like, "I was a legend!" Then she gave me precise instructions on how to walk down from her bedroom through the house into her studio to look inside a specific drawer where she had stored a special, black velvet box that I should bring up to her. So I followed each step and brought up the box—and O M G!—inside glistened the diamond earrings that Oprah had gifted her and all the other legends at the Legends Ball. In and out the box, we basked in the sparkle together.

Gracias a Jesus Por la Oportunidad de Poder
Celebrar mi cumpleaños Nº 35 Con. ElIZABETH CATLETT
"Leyenda del ARTE-AFRO-AMERICANO en MEXICO (en Su Casa
en CUERNAVACA). donde ella desde su cama me regalo
Hermosos cuentos desu vida Maravillosa
GABRIELLE CIVIL  CUERNAVACA. MEXICO 12-OCT-09.

# TUMBLED HISTORIES

"Consider this possibility:
*Casey Florentine's* The Mahavishnu Guide To Lows.
*History re-tumbled to show: Mohandas Ghandi's foray onto
LA's Whittier Blvd shortly before his 1948 assassination.
This under-explored, imaginary episode in the 20th century post-
colonial movement impacted scores of Mexican American youth,
the eventual United Farm Worker's movement, and the appropriation
of South East Asian auto-mobile aesthetics into Chicano."*

Before you try and learn more about Ghandi bumping a lowrider, you should know that this book, *The Mahavishnu Guide To Lows*, does not exist. A certain neo-Aztec trickster named Marco Villalobos invented it as an example of tumbled histories. Marco included this blurb on a flyer for a writing class he taught almost a decade ago. Writing prompts would arrive "via Tumblr posts including: vintage photos, new geographies, library call numbers, word image and sound from the great digital sea as well as from the ancient Dewey decimal system." With its time traveling and intercultural connections, this flyer makes an excellent introduction to Marco.

We met, I think, in Brooklyn in the late nineties. My dear friend Madhu and I had just moved into an apartment building in Prospect Heights and were thrilled to find a poet living right below us. This poet, Vikas Menon, knew how to throw a party. The gathering yielded many life-altering discoveries for me including: 1) There's a laundry room in the building?! 2) I guess I really don't like weed and 3) Marco Villalobos. (Or at least I think Marco surfaced then: the weed thing makes it blurry.) Marco and Vikas were poetry MFA students together at Brooklyn College. I was a grad student in Comp Lit at NYU. Madhu and I were starting to make performance and conceptual art projects with Rosa, the third member of our collective, No 1. Gold. In my memory, Marco, Madhu, Vikas, and I swapped tall tales about the Beats and ancient bards. About hip hop and magic. About moving and shaking in the world.

Tall and lanky, Marco has a sharp mind and an easy smile. He is always ahead of the curve and passionately behind the times. By that I mean, Marco adores the ancient and ancestral. In a recent Spirit Letter, he introduced eighth century Chinese poet Li Po to Russell Jones (aka Ol' Dirty Bastard from the Wu-Tang Clan). He made a film celebrating traditional Son Jarocho music from southern Veracruz. He is a strong proponent of Afro-Mexican culture. "Of course, there are Black people in Mexico," Marco declared. "People need to know. They need to see." Back in 2006, he and photographer Ayanna V. Jackson organized a multi-media traveling exhibit called *African by Legacy, Mexican by Birth*. This was right before I went to Mexico City for the first time. I pored over the pages of this catalogue full of vivid images, and inventive letters, dreaming about Yanga.

# CLARO QUE SÍ

Nothing is better than receiving a letter, even when it doesn't come straight to you.

It's winter in Saint Paul, Minnesota and I'm shivering in my bedroom. As usual, I'm alone, huddled under blankets, swaying my body in time with the oscillating heater so its red coils would always radiate toward my skin. *Riiiiing*. I pick up the phone. It's my mother in Detroit, now relatively balmy in comparison. "An envelope came here for you," she said. That made sense. I had given up my apartment (and my car and many of my belongings) on my sabbatical to world travel the year before, so I had used my parents' address to receive mail.

"It's from the Fulbright Commission.

Do you want me to send it or open it?"

"Open it *right now!*" I respond.

My breath hangs in the air, not just with cold but with hope.

My beating heart generates heat.

"We are pleased to inform you . . ."

The sun breaks through

the other side

of ice and snow

and sparkles across the Mississippi river,

the waves already waving good-bye.

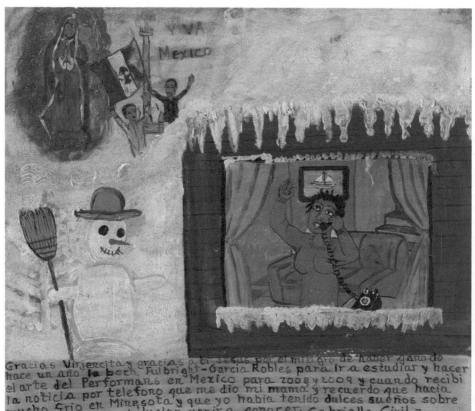

Gracias Virjencita y gracias a ti Jesus por el milagro de haber ganado
hace un año la bech Fulbright-Garcia Robles para ir a estudiar y hacer
el arte del Performans en Mexico para 2008 y 2009 y cuando recibi
la noticia por telefono que me dio mi mama y recuerdo que hacia
mucho frio en Minesota y que yo habia tenido dulces sueños sobre
Mexico, pues era mi ilusion venir a conocer. Gabrielle Civil.-
D.F. 9 de Febrero 2009.

# DEAR MARCO

August 22. 2008
Subject: DF!

Marco!
How awesome to hear from you. Life is so amazing, verdad?
I wasn't even sure if that was your same e-mail but I
wanted to reach out just in case because I know in terms of
Mexico--*you are the man*!

Yes yes--we have a lot to talk about and catch up on. I
haven't even officially started the Fulbright yet--the
orientation is Tuesday--but already it's been a whopping
amazing gift from God. I was able to take a leave from my
job and focus full time on making art and being in the world
and connecting with people and asking questions and figuring
out my life. And dude this money is amazing. They start by
giving you about a quarter of it upfront to help you settle
in. And I really believe if you work it right, it can last
for more than a year.

*  *  *  *  *

Before my trip to Mexico in winter 2007, I had been to
Mexico exactly one time before—to Juarez with Madhu in 1997.
And although I know that's a roughneck city with a history
of violence towards women, etc., we had a magical time and
met some amazing people. So for sabbatical, I knew I wanted
to come back to hang out and work on my Spanish. I spent 10
weeks here-- from January into March 2007--4 in Playa del
Carmen, 1 in Merida (for Carnival), 1 in Guanajuato visiting
a friend and the rest here in Mexico City. (I also got to
visit Elizabeth Catlett in her home in Cuernavaca and swim
in her heated pool, so I can officially die happy.)

Anyway, it just felt like there was this amazing energy here
for me, a kind of opening, something drawing me to come
here. As if there were things for me to do and learn that
could only happen if I dropped what I was doing in other
parts of the world and came back here. The feeling

was esp. powerful because for so much of my life, I'd been
involved with French and chasing Paris and dealing with my
relationship to Haiti and never felt as welcomed in a place
as I did during my brief stint here. So ¡Viva Mexico! I feel
really lucky and also slightly out of place (hence "In and
Out of Place") because when I think of someone like you who
has such a long, deep connection to here, it seems wild for
me to be here (kind of Johnny come lately, you know what I
mean).

So what does, will it mean for me to be here? A couple days
ago, I had an intense conversation with Mónica Mayer and
Victor Lerma, two amazing Mexican performance and conceptual
artists who really jumped on some of my starting art ideas.
(And in another e-mail, we can get into some of that.)
Anyway, Victor's big question for me is "What are you going
to contribute here?" which is such a valid and important
question and one that matters to me greatly. But one I feel
like I'll never be able to answer to his satisfaction.

I told him: I'll be teaching a performance taller through
the museum. Which passed muster. But I also said I'm happy
to be at the service of whoever or whatever needs me.
You're an artist, a member of the performance community
and a Mexican, what do you want me to do? My job is to ask
the community what it is that they want or need and then
do what I can to meet those needs. (Right? This is Freire
101.) And he said: "To come down here and ask what I would

want is unfair." Is it that by already coming, I've negated the choice? Clearly, there is something about "Mexico as the windfall for the gringo" that's at work--as well as the history of incredible Mexican hospitality that ends up with Mexicans getting screwed (rhyming with Haitian history and the whole "New World" . . .)

Anyway, it was a rich, friendly conversation and one that left us all still on good terms. But I left knowing that a lot of this year will necessarily be about me eating shit. You know: not being good enough, not speaking well enough, not having the familial or cultural authority to ever know anything, not ever being able to be right, taking the criticism, displaying humility and having to work hard to prove that I'm not just another gringo asshole. . . .

Or rather, it'll be to eat shit and smile. Because no matter what, I always am delighted to be here. I always know how lucky I am to be here and to get to be here the way that I'm getting to be here: fully paid. And I always have to remember that I am both a guest and one from el otro lado.

For a black person from the US, this is esp. deep because I'm used to having the moral high ground. Having the oppressed history. And I've also been such a smarty pants all my life, I'm used to trusting a working set of knowledge. So to be the dumb one in the room isn't easy. Part of what makes this experience so potentially powerful for me though--as an artist and a person--is how I have to be both humble and strong. How past things are already being thrown out the window . . . How I have to push through old ways of being and also just release and go with the flow.

Anyway, two more things:
1) Mónica  asked Victor--When you lived in the US, what did you give? And he said: Nothing, I was there to get.
2) I said to Victor, one thing that I contribute by being here is the capacity to observe, tell you what I see, ask questions and say back to you what it is that you say. This is a gift not to be underestimated.

Anyway Marco, sorry this is so long! You can see I'm at the start of some deep thinking and making and I wanted to share it with you because I believe that you can appreciate it. What do you think?

Sorry, I haven't even answered some of your basic questions
--so I will next time.  And I'll also take a look at your
footage. I'm off to Spanish class to deal with si hubiera
sido . . .

Abrazos y besos,
Gabrielle

August 23, 2008
Subject: colonias, kiwi & moroccan vodou

Marco aka Illa Lobo-
Wowwwww!
Thanks so much for your kind, thoughtful response to my
last message. It added a cool, generous perspective and
frankly made me feel a lot better. Before I go off in the
next million directions let me say that I'd be happy to be
connected to all of the friends that you mentioned. Feel
free to send them my e-mail and vice versa. I'm hoping to
get a phone here soon, so I'll pass along the number when I
do.

Here's the deal with my living situation.
I'm spending my first month (approx. until Sept. 16) staying
in a place called Casa Tarami, una casa de huéspedes in
Cuauhtémoc not far from the monument El Ángel.

I stayed here for a month last year and love the owners
Gabriel and Katy. They are very kind and welcoming and
speak 5 languages (so we alternate between French, Spanish
and English). It's very posh--individual studio apartments
with wifi and cable. A nice way to transist from the US I
suppose--but definitely a splurge. It's much too expensive
for me to stay for the entire year. So I have about 3 weeks
to find a place to live. If you have any suggestions about
colonias or any friends who might be looking for a roommate,
housesitter, etc.--lemme know.  (Your friends in Turkey with
the apartment here sound verrrrry intriguing . . . ;-) )

In the meantime, I'm not too stressed about living
conditions because I feel like 3 weeks is enough time to
find something and I'm not very picky about where I live.
I'd prefer not to live too far south (Coyoacán, etc.)
because it seems a little suburban and chi chi and everyone
says the Condesa and Polanco are so great, but they seem a
little bcbg yuppy to me too . . . But I just want a place
that's safe, somewhat central and gets some light. I don't
need a lot of space, I don't need to live alone, and I don't
want to spend a lot of money.

A bigger issue for me will be where to work (write, make and show art). I'm realizing that if I'm to live and work in the same space, I'll either need two rooms or a larger studio. I have * a lot* of work of various kinds to do right now (revising and developing my book, performance video editing, etc.) and I find myself flopped out, eating kiwi and watching the Olympics and reruns of "El ley y la orden" . . . WTF! **Amigo, that will not do for my year of art, solidarity and self improvement!** ;-)

When I was heading off to my Spanish class each morning, I had such an itch to stay home and write and do stuff. But today when I could do it, I felt so lazy. I'll chalk it up to the altitude. (Yeah, right.) Monday, I get to have coffee and chocolates with Lorena Wolffer, another lovely Mexican performance artist that I met last time. (Another day, I'll tell you the story about how her 2 year old daughter Kira hid their home phone in my purse, only to be discovered by me later when I was reaching in to pay a bill at a coffee shop. Oh--I guess I just told you the story.)

The rest of next week is dominated by the Fulbright Orientation. Elena Poniatowska is coming to talk about the 1968 student massacres. (And Mónica Mayer said something really interesting about that and all the commemorations of the Revolution that they're doing this year. She said: "I don't celebrate wars. It would be like celebrating when your father beat your mother. These things are shameful and not to be remembered in public. We should celebrate the times we almost went to war and didn't." Interesting perspective, no?) They also have lectures on Mexican history, a trip to Teotihuacan and a cocktail party at the embassy (for which I will be wearing a pretty stunning white dress with turquoise spaghetti straps--stand back!) Good luck again on your application--my fingers are crossed.

Gracias, Saludos, and Abrazos,
Gabrielle

September 2, 2008
Subject: sinergia!

Marco! Polo!
I'm not sure if things are rolling along in el DF but tons
of stuff certainly is happening. The Fulbright Orientation
was jam packed (I don't want to tell you too much so you
will have surprises--knock on wood--but suffice it to say
that they demonstrated the Mexican man-pat greeting. That
emblematizes one level of the proceedings. But they did have
Sergio Aguayo talk about human rights. He was good--but I
wish Elena Poniatowska could have come . . .)

Oh and the turquoise spaghetti strap event went well. All
the rest of me was a sheath of white and the great thing was
that no one else was wearing white at all. Almost all of the
women were wearing black. (And most of the women were white,
so it made a nice poetic reversal. ;-) ) It was out in the
Beverly Hills part of the DF and they didn't have much food
but they did have gin. You did have to pass by a person with
a gun to get in the door though (this reminded me of my
aunt's house in Haiti) so all in all I don't think I'll be
applying for diplomatic service anytime soon . . .

I went to an opening last night at the Alameda--a media art
show with good energy and met a lot of nice people. It was
called Sinergia and that's a little of how I feel. Lots of
energy flowing with lots of things. I feel like I want to
clone myself just to see and do all the cool stuff around
here.

Is it true that you don't like el DF?
Or is it just that places like Southern Veracruz call more
to your soul? . . .
In the meantime, I'm supposed to have lunch with este Daniel
H tomorrow. He also sent me a link to an opening for the
work of Rirkrit Tiravanija whom I love . . . But I think it
conflicts with a trip to a bar with another Fulbrighter to
hang out with octogenarian ex-boxers from Cuba. I'll let you
know how it goes.

I'm off kiwi and on to tangerines--
All the best to you and yours--
Gabrielle

September 7, 2008
Subject: everybody ñ

Dear Marco aka my US Pen Pal:
Thanks so much for your last message. I especially loved
the images of you waiting tables (like Langston Hughes),
breaking wine glasses and installing breathalyzers. Anything
for a buck, brother indeed! Everything for creativity and
joy.

It's nice to have a poet to write to . . . I just got
after one of my best friends--a business guy with an artist
heart-- about his terse, vague e-mails. He writes things
like "Things are good, just busy." What does that mean? It
turns out that his home computer is broken and so he's had
to e-mail from work which is heavily surveilled. I just hope
the incoming messages aren't scanned too. (I was telling
him about this great videoperformance I watched called
"Masturbating in the Fatherland"--it featured the younger
male artist, an older gentleman playing guitar and singing a
canción, and a nice fresh carrot.) ;-)

Did I tell you that I was asked to be on the jury for a
videoperformance show at Ex Teresa? I feel really honored
to have been asked. There are over a hundred submissions--
each up to 10 minutes--so I've been watching a really varied
bunch of short performances for the camera. It's been a real
spur to my own creativity. Sometimes I look at art and it's
so beautiful and thoughtful and well executed that I wonder
who on earth am I to even try to do it. Other times, I
look at things and wonder--is this what's getting over?
C'mon . . . The best times are when I look at something and
it's lovely and it both inspires and invites me. It seems to
be asking: What are you waiting for . . .

Just as I've been judging one show, I've been trying to
get into another one. There's something called the Eject
Videoperformance festival started by a great guy called
Pancho López. I wanted to submit some earlier stuff but left
the right mini-DVs at home. :-( --So I just decided: I have
a camera, I just bought a new Mac for the purpose of making
videos so let's get to it. I had less than a week before the
deadline and so it was like an instant art project.

What made it hard is that I'm really familiar with the old
I-movie, but the new version is a nightmare. It took me
twice as long to edit my footage—and you know editing takes
three times as long as shooting. (I know you're a million
times more advanced than me with film but please still feel
my pain.) Anyway, I put together a minute and a half video
called "Here Come the Whites!" There's some shuckin, jiving
and lots of teeth. It's part of some ongoing video work I've
been doing with close-ups. And it's the first in a series
I'm working on now called "Meditations on Slavery." I'm not
sure how original any of this stuff is, but you have to be
we're you're at, ya know.

In the meantime, the last couple days here have been
absolutely magical. Yesterday, I was on the Metrobús on
Insurgentes and saw the most intense thing. There was a
demonstration near the Reforma stop. I had been taking
pictures earlier of the protest posters but on the Metrobús
I saw something amazing. Dozens of men and women were all
wearing cowboy hats and stomping and shouting and singing.
And they were all naked except for a photo of a slain
man hung over their genitalia. And encircling them was a
ring of police with guns, their backs rigid against the
protestors' movement. And I couldn't tell if the police were
turning their back to what had happened or somehow posturing
protection for those brown naked bodies. INTENSE. I wish I
had hung out there longer . . .

Speaking of long, I'm sorry this is such a book. Let me
cut to the last exciting thing: I met Daniel Hernandez!
who is good people--> so thanks for the contact. And
he represented for "his girl Daf" hardcore--so let her
know that he's sending love to her worldwide. We met at
this gallery opening for an artist I usually love named
Rirkrit Tiravanija. Do you know that guy? Daniel actually
interviewed him and I'd love to know more what he said.
I wasn't so into the work that night. It was supposedly
a meditation on the tropical--but what should have been
poetic and minimal and figurative and elegant felt a little
empty and absent. Or maybe just obvious. Like he needed to
be pushed harder. Or maybe I would have liked it more if
it wasn't such a fancy schmancy opening . . . Tons of hip,
artsy folk with thick black glasses and funky shoes . . .
Yowza . . .

Rirkrit did install the place with tons of palm plants.
And we all got t-shirts (some of which said Menos Petroleo
Mas Valor--see what I mean?) and there was beer and Boingos
and fresh heavy cocos and a woman with the most amazing
fake nails painted brown who hacked the cocos open with a
machete. She was the best thing about the night for me. How
she cut triangles in the cocos and stuck in the straw. And
how after you drank all the water, she'd hack them open and
cut out the flesh and add chili and lime . . . I guess if
Rirkrit brought that to the art world, I can't be too mad at
him. Ok, send me your address so I can send you a copy of
these video sketches.

I'd be curious to get your opinion.
Abrazos!
Gabrielle

Surround Sound.

Ambience.

Establishing Shot.

White Tiles on the Floor.

Nobody.

Close-Up.

My Dusky Brown Feet.

Ashy.

Percussive Thudding.

Humming.

More Like

Breathy Whistle.

Close-Up.

A Corn Straw Broom.

Shucking and Sweeping.

YESSUH!

Clouds of Dust.

Entering the Frame.

My Dusky Brown Face.

Close-Up.

Here Come The Whites!

Bulging Eyeballs.

Inflated Cheeks.

Chiclet Teeth.

Ghost Grin.

We Wear the _____

Reset.

Do It Again.

With Your Face.

From Stoic Resting.

Ready?

Bugged Eye Spook.

One Last Time.

One Minute

& Thirty-Six Seconds.

Centuries.

Blackout.

The Word Slavery.

The End.

# HERE COME THE WHITES!

Nobody liked *Here Come the Whites!* Or if they did, nobody said so. It was the first video I made in Mexico City, probably my first month there, and it showed in the 2008 *EJECT* videoperformance festival a few months later. That may have been the only time it was shown, although maybe it played in my disastrous "In & Out of Place" gallery show a couple years later in Minnesota. I can't remember. In fact, when I replayed the video just now, after writing about it from memory, it turns out that my memory had slipped after so many years. The video actually starts with my face, already eye-rolling, growing into a sarcastic smile. Then like a B-movie horror flick, the title jumps out on the screen.

*Here Come the Whites!*

What did that mean in Mexico City?

Figures of the body were on my mind, figures of self, postures of history. I had a grandiose idea to make a series called "Meditations on Slavery." This would be videos of me skirting the line between stereotypical and iconic African American gestures. *Here Come the Whites!* would be the first one. (*Here Come the Whites!* ended up being the only one I ever made.) The technology was a struggle. Remember the first I-movie? It was so easy to use. I'd camped out in the faculty lab and cut reels and burned DVDs to project original videos in my performances or make work samples for grant applications. Finally, right before coming to Mexico, I'd saved up to buy my very own Mac laptop, only to realize that I was now in a different country and didn't know how to use the new terrible I-movie and had to learn it on my own and troubleshoot the interface between my video camera and my new computer with different electricity and adapters. Looking back, this marked the start of my ongoing battle against obsolescence, but I rallied to make this tiny movie. *Here Come the Whites!* runs a little more than a minute and a half, but it took hours for me to make. It felt like a threshold: starting to make work in Mexico City, running into resistance, and trying to figure it out. The process exhilarated me. It also started me getting used

31

to another important thing. Mexican audiences don't mince words. At least not with me.

"I know you from that video," one cool chica said to me at a party. "I didn't like it." Here we go. My stoic resting face didn't crack. She went on, "You know, you have some talent. You could be like, wait, what's her name? ¡KARA WALKER! Yes, you should do something like that." Yes, I agreed. Kara Walker is amazing. I didn't roll my eyes. Just listened. Even La Congelada herself who had been so congratulatory the night of the premiere, "Yay! Gabrielle you're in the festival!" Later, in private, she said. "Gabrielle, that video was NADA! NADA!" Was it really so bad? Or did they just want something so much more from me?

Sergio Peña intimated as much when we first met. Sergio, fluent in Scandinavian languages because, after watching the Lillehammer Olympics as a boy in sultry Tamaulipas, Sergio had dreamed of snow and so studied in Norway and Sweden and gained a Swedish momma and papa, even Sergio said, "Yes, I did see that video of yours. Really, I thought it could have been a lot better."

# Gabrielle Civil O El Arte De No Pasar De Largo
## por Sergio Peña

Si tuviera la necesidad de presentar México a un extranjero de la manera más cercana y afectiva posible recurriría a una artista norteamericana (sí): Gabrielle Civil (Detroit, MI). Nada más honesto y palpitante que su interpretación de emociones y atmósferas mexicanas. Es increíble la efectividad con que esta artista, que residió en la Ciudad de México poco más de un año, ha logrado transmitir al espectador su experiencia mexicana valiéndose de todos los recursos a su alcance: danza, voz, música de mariachi, imágenes en video, aromas (a flores, frutas), besos, abrazos, sabores, ritmo, cantos a capella, así como juegos de palabras bilingües dónde se libera una poesía cargada de idiosincrasia fonética.

Conocí a Gabrielle por destino más que por accidente. En 2008 tuvo lugar, en el Museo Ex Teresa de la Ciudad de México, una exhibición de videoperformance con artistas de varios países. Un trabajo breve y que, a decir verdad, no me causó mayor impresión fue mi primer contacto con Gabrielle. Se trató de un video dónde el trabajo principal lo realizaba su rostro, ese rostro expresivo que posteriormente apreciaría tanto ver. Las palabras que decía ese rostro en el video no dejaron huella en mí, pero el rostro en sí lo hizo: contenía una energía inusual, era como si ese solo rostro, de haberlo querido, hubiera podido hacer reír o llorar a los espectadores a su antojo… Pero me pareció que no tuvo ganas de hacerlo en ese trabajo, o tal vez–como estuve convencido más tarde–no estuvo consciente de que podía hacerlo.

33

Pocas veces se tiene la oportunidad de comunicarle al artista personalmente la opinión que se tiene acerca de una obra suya. Pues, en mi caso, esa oportunidad llegó pocos días después de haber visto el video de Gabrielle; inesperadamente, durante una fiesta en casa de una amiga común cuando, entre la gente, apareció ese rostro energético que me era tan familiar… Gabrielle escuchó mi comentario y pude ver cómo su rostro expresivo se ponía serio y concentrado, me escuchaba de manera profunda y nada superficial (como bien pudo haber hecho, sobre todo porque se trataba de un comentario que cuestionaba el resultado de un trabajo suyo).

Gabrielle agradeció el comentario y desde ese instante supe que había más, mucho más detrás de ese rostro que dejó de serme familiar para serme entrañable. Mi curiosidad por su trabajo se disparó y durante su año en México tuve la fortuna de ser testigo de primera línea de la evolución que tomó su trabajo.

# Gabrielle Civil or The Art of Leaving an Imprint
## by Sergio Peña
## Translated by Lucía Abolafia Cobo

If I had to introduce Mexico City to a foreigner in the most accurate and emotional way, I would turn to an American artist (yes): Gabrielle Civil (Detroit, MI). There is nothing more honest and vibrant than her interpretation of Mexican emotions and atmospheres. It's amazing how effectively this artist, who lived in Mexico City for just over a year, managed to convey her Mexican experience to the viewer by using all possible means at hand: dancing, voice, Mariachi music, video images, scents (flowers, fruits), kisses, hugs, flavors, rhythm, a capella songs and bilingual puns where a poetry full of phonetic idiosyncrasies is released.

It was by fate rather than by accident that I met Gabrielle. In 2008, a video performance exhibition with artists from several other countries took place at the Ex Teresa Museum in Mexico City. It was through a brief performance art piece—that, to be honest, did not leave a great impression on me—that I first met Gabrielle. The work presented was a video where the focus was her face—an expressive face that later on I came to appreciate so much.

The words said in the video left no impression on me, but rather her face did: it contained an unusual energy, one that could have made the viewers laugh or cry to its own sway—if only it would have wanted to—. But I thought she did not have the wish to do so in that performance, or perhaps—as I later came to realize—she was not aware she could do so.

36

Only very few times does the opportunity arise to communicate personally to artists what you think about their work. Well, in my case such opportunity arose just a few days after having seen Gabrielle's video. I was at a house party of a friend we have in common when unexpectedly that energetic face, that was so familiar to me, appeared... Gabrielle listened to my comments. I saw her expressive face become serious and focused—she was intently listening to me and did not seem at all shallow (as she very well could have been given the fact that my comments were questioning the result of one of her works).

Gabrielle appreciated the comments and from that moment on, I knew there was more, much more behind that face that stopped being so familiar and started to be so endearing. Her work detonated my curiosity and during the year she stayed in Mexico I was lucky enough to witness the evolution of her work from the first row.

October 1, 2008
Subject: portrait of the artist as a strawberry

Hola Marco amiguito!
Thank you so much for your wonderful message. I hope that
grant writing season has treated you well, along with the
deconstruction of the furniture and the reconstruction of
the furniture (Louise Bourgeois would be proud) for the
visit of Daffodil's family. Did you all have fun with the
folks? I could practically smell the food simmering on the
stove . . .

You both will be happy to know that just last night I
was over at Daniel Hernandez' "sick" pad in el Centro
celebrating the birthday of lil Will, a kid from all around
America who just turned 20 years old. Can you imagine? At
the fiesta were ex pat journalists, Mexican make-up artists
and photographers, a Brit jazz singer, a folkloric dancer
and Daniel's boyfriend Uriel and his friend Daniela (who
were my favorites). Daniel and I are talking about having
some writing sessions together. A draft of his book is due
in Dec. and my draft is due forever ago so maybe we can help
each other motivate.

In the meantime, let me get real real and speak to you of
the realities of realty here in the DF. Daniel's apartment
is exactly the kind of place I dreamed of being able to
find in Mexico City. Not too big--but with a bedroom,
pretty wooden floors, lots of light, buen ambiente and hella
cheap (about half of what I'm about to pay--more about that
later). He looks out his window and sees "Iluminación,"
the "Techno Lite" lighting store and a vitrine of modern
chandeliers. He said it took a while to find and he had to
jump through a lot of hoops and he doesn't have a fridge or
much furniture--but it's really amazing. In the Centro close
to the Alameda which may not be a location for beginners to
the City--but really shows me what someone can do here in
the DF (hats off to Daniel!) Although as an extranjera, it's
not at all what I did . . .

Cut to Gabriela la Cazadora de Departamentos--a new monument
coming to the Reforma 2009! After more than a month of
being in Mexico City, I finally sucked it up and found an

apartment. It's quite charming--full of light and wooden
floors. It belonged to the grandmother of my soon-to-
be landlady (herself a successful playwright here named
Leonor Azcarate). And I will be the first tenant post-
abuela. It has two bedrooms--one of which I will use for
a studio and lots of long halls to hang up art and images
and experiments. When I saw it, it had no meubles, but
she is furnishing it for me for a little more money. (This
is a leap of faith of course, because I have no idea what
those meubles will look like.) Still somehow when I walked
into the space, I felt like it was meant to be mine . . .
Everything is brand new. Clean. Shiny. A space
of possibility.

But it's a lot more money that I wanted to spend. I feel
kind of bougie . . . or as they say here all the time:
fresa. When I first arrived, I really wanted to live
with some Mexican grad students or young professionals to
save money, improve my Spanish and have a more "local"
experience. There are a bunch of Fulbrighters who live
in the Condesa and who only hang out there and surround
themselves with other ex-pats or each other and I swore to
myself that I wouldn't be like that. And I'm not. BUT I can
see I am a little strawberry. Because when I had a chance to
live a little high on the hog (i.e. alone, with extra space
for guests and work and art-making in a neighborhood that's
pretty secure), I took it. It's more than I wanted to pay,
but I can afford it. But I still feel a little weird . . .
So before I pick up the keys from the landlady tomorrow, let
me take this metaphysical moment:

What does it mean to live in a place? What does it meant to
afford a place? What does it mean to make art in a place?
What does it mean to live as an artist? How does one afford
it? What does it mean to be able to afford it?

Even more than writing, I feel like performance requires
space for the body and movement . . . But at the same time,
there is something about being in a place, eating, walking,
connecting with people that should happen in order for art
to come into and from that place . . . I think this is why
and how my apartment hunting became such a comic struggle.
There were so many values I felt like I was trying to
balance. And my Libran whiplash shifts about money are also
deeply worked into it all too.

Anyway, I don't know who Leonor's abuela was but her energy
made me feel so welcome that I have to trust that I'm doing
the right thing. And just enjoy the place. Fill it with
flowers and friends. Claim it as an open space of creativity
and thinking and being. An afforded privilege and a gift.
It's in the Roma on Coahuila between Monterrey and Medellín,
close to the Campeche Metrobus on Insurgentes and the
Chilpancingo metro station. It's right next to a beautiful
fruit and vegetable market. And I'd be happy for you and
Daffodil to come and visit sometime.

In the meantime, I still haven't transferred the rest of
my microperformances the way I planned. I think my video
quality is kind of crappy--but I think it would still be
worthwhile to finish the documentation of my "Meditations on
Slavery" series. So once I get into my new place that's one
of the things I plan to do.

And I'll send it to you along with a few other things of
interest. I also want to look at the footage I shot from El
Grito. I did go to the Zócalo and had a wonderful time. Ate
pozole on 5 de Sept. Walked through metal detectors. Danced
to cumbia in the rain. And also got to experience the double
experience of López Obrador on one side and Calderón on
the other. What is your view of this whole conflict? I was
amazed that López Obrador even got to be there (could you
imagine Bush sharing the floor with Gore?)!

Now that the election is about a month away, what is your view of things? Esp. from the great state of California? My absentee ballot just arrived in MN and I'm having people international priority it here and I'm going to international priority it back! This election is so huge, I can't let it go down without me. Need I say: Barack the Vote!

Okay, sorry again this is so long. And thanks for the contact with Carlos! We've been trying to get together-- he plans to cook me food. Yum . . . Indulge me with one last crazy story. My friend Jennifer lives in an apartment in the Condesa that she sublet from her friend of a friend Brad. In this apartment is a huge painting of two indigenous astronauts doing a ceremony in space. Jennifer said that her friend Brad's friend Carlos who lives in Tlalpan painted this painting. I was looking at this painting in Brad's now Jennifer's apartment when your friend Carlos who lives in Tlalpan called me on the phone. We were chatting and Jennifer said--Carlos lives in Tlalpan? I bet he's the same Carlos who did the painting. I said: that's nuts! There have to be a million Carloses in Tlalpan. This isn't Cleveland. She said: ask him. So, I said: "Carlos, eres pintor?" "Sí." "Tienes un amigo que se llama Brad?" "Sí." "Tienes un cuadro en su depa?" "Sí." Completely nonchalant! I said, Carlos--do you have a lot of paintings in apartments in the Condesa? He said No. And I said--well don't you think it's crazy that I would be looking right now at the one you have here? And we both laughed.

Anyway, does this mean you know Brad too? And have been to his palacio? Okay pal. Slowly but surely, I'm starting to settle into this big, bad beautiful city. Drop a line when you get a chance.

Cheers,
Gabrielle

October 11, 2008
Subject: champaña (98% angst free)

Dear Marco—
Thank you so much for your lovely message. The pictures were
especially wonderful and imbued with synchronicity. There's
no internet yet in my new apartment and so I was over at
el Palacio Condechi de Brad (now de la Hennifer) drinking
orange juice freshly squeezed in the old school juicer from
green oranges bought at the Tuesday market when I opened
your e-mail.

How crazy!
And how sublime all four of you looked atop the roof! Each
of you in a different world, but all with champagne. The
world is indeed a tumbler of water. And I can't wait to hear
more about you and Brad and the Berlin-grassovska anarchist
hole in the wall. Although I must say—bloody marys. Ugh!
Gimme a mimosa for brunch or a gin and tonic any day . . .
Next time, next time . . .;-)

Speaking of champagne, tomorrow is my birthday! So last
night, I bought 5 bottles of champagne, a lemon panque and
a case of Indio to have some folks over. You'll be happy
to know both Daniel H and Carlos Cons are on the guest
list, as well as an assorted group of Fulbright fellows,
Mexican performance artists, and people I've met in bars, at
openings or on the street. A ver! On my possible shopping
list today: a hula hoop, a piñata, some tarot or lotéria
cards, a pinwheel and a game I saw featured at Juegetron
last week: "100 Mexicanos Dicen." Apparently, I don't trust
organic fun or the social compatibility of my acquaintances.
Bring on the games! And the booze of course.

I almost wasn't going to have a get-together at all for
my birthday. As my e-mails can attest, my moods have been
swinging wildly here in el Distrito Federal. How angsty I
have been! Good Lord! Did I tell you? A week and a half
ago, I actually woke up in a cold sweat in the middle of the
night about the quality of my work and the direction of my
life. What the fuck?! That's never been me. And right now,
I have a paid fellowship to make art in Mexico City for a

year—so why have I been feeling less carefree than ever?
Self-imposed pressure? Early midlife crisis? Just getting
older? I don't know—but it's certainly taken me aback.
Hopefully, this next year I will be New & Improved: 98%
angst free. (With 2% left for the rich "metaphysical dilemma
of being black and a woman" as Shange would say).

In my last day of angst, then—ahem—let me say, the problem
is magic.

I have always believed in magic and this is a risky thing
because it demands openness while acknowledging chaos. Plus
it raises the standard of living pretty high. Magic is the
spell of the poem, or the way the sky can change or how
Thursday was the Anniversario del Mercado Medellín and on
a tiny bandshell, an 8 piece salsa band rocked out in the
middle of the afternoon and people from all walks of life—
including me—danced and ate food and cake and laughed and
how I could just stumble into it.  But the flipside is just
stumbling. Recognizing that at any moment, it could go any
way—lovely or cruel or just endlessly expectant—and maybe
the magical moments can only go so far. What if it's more
about the two words you mentioned a couple times in your
last e-mail: luck and chance? Or even fate? I guess I don't
believe that my happiness is completely in my control.
Which is both terrifying and a relief . . .

Tomorrow anyway, I'll give it a shot. I'll bring people
together, get drunk and eat cake. ;-) Hopefully, this will
be magical . . . Maybe it will be enough for now. At least,
I'll have tried. And as my grandmother would say—I'll give
the rest up to Jesus!

And speaking of hope, trying, and Jesus: I know, I know,
Barack has been mild and stiff of late. I didn't see the
debates, but it doesn't seem like his best forum. He is not
hip hop. As much as we might want, he does not and will not
BaRock the Mic. He's more 1960s cool pose. I can see him
wearing a shiny suit and a thin dark tie, carrying a record
case into the party. It totally makes sense that he wanted
"Hold On! I'm Comin'" as his campaign song. Still, he is a
compromiser, not a firebrand, but, I believe, a good guy and
as you know hella better than the alternative. I can only
pray that through the grace of God, the spirits, the roots
and the streets, he will win this election. My absentee

ballot is en route to me here via UPS; I am determined to cast my vote...

Oh and how much is a catalogue for your exhibit? If there are any left, I'd love to have one. I want to learn more about el tercer raíz. Let me know what else is going on in the angst-free paradise of Long Beach. . . What are you listening to? What are you looking at? What are you reading? Please give my best to your flower Daffodil!

Cheers,
Gabrielle

November 19, 2008
Subject: get ready for the smack down (!)

Querido amigo Marco,
How lovely to hear from you. Perhaps it's true that the
universe gives us what we need--for you, the sun, the ash,
the smell of fire, the slow cooked ox-tails, wine (!), agua
de jamaica with lime (!), a six foot cleaver, friends,
memories and daily creative thoughts. I sat down to do some
homework (!) for my performance taller, feeling completely
uninspired, and your e-mail has given me a nice creative
boost.

At times, Mexico is hard.

Maybe if my people were from here--or appear in more than
five minute bursts on a city street in which me and another
dark-skinned Sally or Sam practically embrace--it would
be a little easier. Or maybe, if I weren't such a busy bee
running from thing to thing and let myself relax, rest,
ground myself a little more in the rhythms of this amazing
city, I would feel a little less cast out. Or also maybe,
if I hadn't stepped back in the United States of Obama last
week and felt so optimistic, so spectacularly competent--nay
brilliant--at daily life (tooling a car around destinations
I know by  heart, speaking a language in a straight shot
between thought and word, walking onto my campus like a
returning rock star, a bit undercover but gleam radiating
through), I'd feel more at home today.

Last month, I met a Haitian guy named Slyjine who had
come to Mexico to work and make his life better. A couple
weeks later, I saw him again on the street and he said
"Je retourne à l'Haïti le 4 de novembre." "Pourquoi?" I
asked. "Parce quien Haïti, je suis architecte y ici je suis
*nada.*" Ouch! It's not that deep for me--I'm not nada here.
And I've moved away somewhat from the early jitters of angst
I felt before--but this stretch I definitely feel the step
down from architect to zip.

So much has been going on!
Cold weather, my bad cold, cold shoulders in my questionable
relationships with Mexican men.

45

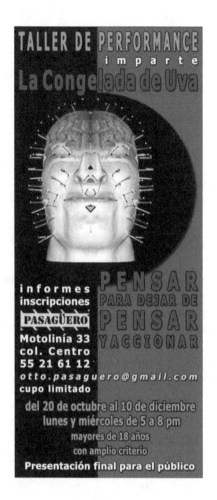

The biggest thing though has to do with this performance workshop that I'm taking which may or may not have been the best thing. Call it my Booker T. Washington moment. Training, son. I'm always after training.

And although I know a bunch of performance artists here, these first months I really craved a home creative environment, an artistic community to help me organize my time, produce new work and learn more about philosophy and production of performance art here in Mexico City. Sounds good, right? Well, I said from the start that far from the shiny penny, I've been the dull centavo here, and it seems like everything I do for this workshop isn't good enough!

# MY FROZEN GRAPE TEACHER

Grape Frozen Bombe Pop

Grape Monster Pop or Sugar Pop

Grape Fla-Vor-Ice or Tast-ee Freeze

Lady Grape Popsicle

Female Frozen Grape Thing

Honorific Thing to Suck

Something Cold that Burns Sweet

The Grape Icee

\*

La Congelada de Uva is hard to translate. Along with Mónica Mayer and Lorena Wolffer, she was one of the Mexican women artists I met on that first trip to Mexico City in 2007. Her name appeared on the list that Édith Medina gave me in the Centro de Documentacíon at Ex Teresa. One of the most famous contemporary performance artists in Mexico, she explores sex, gender and the erotic in her work. She explodes taboos to resist the repression of women. La Congelada loves to play with her vagina. I mean literally. She's tied up her legs and eaten sushi pulled from her twat. To advocate for human rights, she played a concert on her "pussyphone" ("pepáfono"). To satirize the virgin/whore dichotomy, she dressed up like a nun, stuck a small baby Jesus up her pussy, and sewed it shut. At least, that's what I heard. Rumors say she had to be rushed to the hospital to get it out. Lots of rumors swirl around La-con-hey! That she's a freak. That she's a man-eater. That she loves orgies and blood. Pain and Porn. Shock and awe. That she turned herself into a giant fuck cyborg. That in one performance, she was fucked live for hours while she scrubbed the floor. That she went to the Zócalo, the public square in downtown Mexico City, and shat on images of Mexican President Enrique Peña Nieto. Apparently Mexican Twitter blew up. Is that art? Who the hell is this crazy woman?

48

Born Rocío Boliver in 1956, she studied philosophy and dance. She writes articles, porno-erotic reflections, and has worked in theater and video. Tall, thin, and blond with high cheekbones and hazel eyes, she has also worked as a fashion model and television presenter. She embodies Eurocentric beauty standards and throws them out the window. She's not afraid to be ugly, crude, aggressive, intense, or hypersexual. Some say her stage name La Congelada de Uva came from one performance where she masturbated live with a grape popsicle. The name also lampoons feminine ideals, self-censorship, the need for anonymity to talk about sex, and the self-seriousness of Mexican cultural elites. In the pantheon of performance art, she'd be like the Mexican Annie Sprinkle with shades of Karen Finley, Madonna, and Ron Athey. La Congelada is hardcore. She can also be very warm and funny.

Back in 2007, we met at the Salon de Corona, chatted, and drank beers and she told me about her work. To my delight, she invited me to drop in on a performance art *taller* (or workshop) that she was teaching at Ex Teresa. A group of about ten students gathered, mostly in their twenties, to explore the possibilities of el Arte Actual. One guy got naked and rubbed meat all over his body. One woman sang and shook. An older man instructed a young volunteer to take off her clothes and lie down while he administered rituals over her body. Rigorous and audacious, La Congelada presided firmly over the room. Rock music played. People danced. What would it be like to study performance art in a class like that?

La Congelada smiled.

# ON TALLER

*(What is the training of an artist?*
*Disposition gives desire. Talent would make it easier.*
*Hard work is unavoidable for even those with the first two.*
*Training is something else: a more methodical way of*
*approaching, considering and developing a body of knowledge.)*

Although it can stretch you and make you grow, *taller* is not pronounced taller. The Spanish word for workshop sounds closer in English to *tie air*. This aligns with the often enigmatic tasks we are called to do in La Congelada de Uva's performance art taller.

Do a simple action for three minutes.

Have others watch you.

Alter your body in a way that is subtle but unsettling in public.

Walk across the room without walking.

Tell your life story in a language that doesn't exist.

Do something transgressive in public.

Open a dictionary (of philosophy, of slang, of myth, etc.) at random.

Read an entry aloud. Forget the specifics.

Make a performance with the gist.

Get angry with someone who has done nothing to deserve it.

Take it as far as it goes.

Wake up in the morning and put stones in your shoes.

Walk around with them all day.

Select an object that has sentimental value to you.

Destroy it.

Research and present on the work of a performance artist.

Listen to a chapter on the history of performance art read aloud.

Go to a specialty shop and make a performance

with things that you find there

Make a performance using your bodily fluids.

Tell a story from your childhood for three minutes

the way you would tell it as a child.

Do this completely naked.

Create an estampa congelada, a tableau vivant in which you will be the center.

Decide on one specific gesture. Repeat this gesture in set rhythm over time.

Write up a full application to present a performance action you have never done.

List all of your setting, lighting, and technical requirements.

Write out every gesture of your piece with as much detail as possible.

Walk 150 steps away from where we are now.

Make a performance from something you find there.

With others, untangle an extremely tangled ball of twine.

Then be wrapped with them in the same twine you unraveled.

11/19/08 cont.

Sorry again Marco to make you be my shrink / big brother.
But for a few minutes, I'm going to take advantage of your
electronic couch / shoulder.

Let's start with the chicken bones. For the second class, we
had to transform an object on / and our person to create an
effect that was subtle and wasn't immediately disconcerting.
You weren't supposed to be obvious--i.e. it shouldn't look
like you were out to capture attention. Rather there was
supposed to be something about you that when you caught
another person's eye, they would immediately be bothered--
kind of like when an insect comes into your field and you
swat it away before you even know what it is.

This is actually a great exercise for a performance artist--
although a hard one (and already with a kind of negative
undertone that's different from my approach). And so what I
did was take some frozen chicken that my friend was keeping
for stock and boil it down to the bones and then take thin
red copper wire to fasten a necklace. I can't tell you how
much I enjoyed the process of making that necklace. The ride
over to my friend's house, the boiling down, the talk to the
guy at the hardware store, the washing of the bones, the
winding of the ends and the way I had to hold my neck just
so to ensure that it would stay. Even as I was making it, I
wondered: is this stereotypical . . .? Am I just reinforcing
some black exotic thing like when I knowingly wear zebra
stripes? But my time was short and I'd made my decision and
I made my necklace and I loved it.

Of course, it didn't go over at all.

No one got a good review on the exercise actually. Jere wrote "Tengo genes defectivos, entonces soy divino y perfecto" in black marker on a white t-shirt which La Congelada, our teacher, said was too obvious and flat. Bele, a young goth girl, wore a pink dress and tights and a religious pin with a Saint, and la Conge said that unless we already knew Bele, it wasn't disconcerting at all. The person who came closest was Ore (look at these names-- Jere, Bele, Ore, la Conge and Gabrielle--and see how I'm already set up to feel like an outsider). He, a grown man, took the train with a stuffed animal seal stuffed in his shirt. Although she said that stuffing the seal in the shirt took it a step too far, the overall effect of a grown man with a child's toy was a little weird. With me, she said: Gabrielle, you already said why this doesn't work. "Tú eres africana y todos saben que los africanos comen los niños. Entonces, no hay efecto de nada."

Clearly, she's being sarcastic. And I don't disagree with her assessments, but this exercise spoke to a lot of dynamics for me about being "in and out of place," making performance art in Mexico City, and also in that taller.

It's a rough trick to arrive already out of context, to
not fully know or understand the context, and then try
to disrupt quotidian life. I can't complain about that
because it is the heart of my project--although I'm more
about opening space than disrupting life. What I came
to understand is that my art making has a lot to do with
process and ritual and that something in me likes to make
the strange beautiful and the beautiful strange. This was
a nice thing to realize. But it also puts me at odds with
what she's setting us up to do. She wants us to be warriors,
disturbers of the peace, if I'm generous I would say
tricksters, or if I'm not I'd say assholes.

Next exercise: do some kind of transgression in public.
Again, you know I'm a good girl. And also being visibly
different in someone else's country is not for me the best
scenario for public transgression--but again, I understand
the rationale for the exercise. Performance artists need
to be unafraid of transgression. We have to move outside
of the box. And the transgression needn't be big. Go to
McDonald's and order chicken and mole, she said. Go to the
subway and tell them that you lost your ticket and ask the
guard to pass. Being extranjera, these are the kinds of
transgressions I do everyday without even meaning to (!).
But still it was rough to think about what exactly I'd do
because I didn't want to cause anyone trouble. For example,
when I asked Ore what he would do, he said: I'll just take
some eggs and throw them at a window. For me, that's so
fucked up. Because all I could see was some brown-skinned
woman having to pull out a mop and clean it up. (Am I too
soft-hearted to be a hard-core performance artist?)

I went to an América-Chivas football match and at half time
went to the men's bathroom instead of the women's bathroom.
This kind of transgression felt right to me because the
social rule is arbitrary, no one got hurt (although many
were bewildered and amused), and also the women's line was
hella long and I had to pee. . .

Okay, now the big kahuna. For the next exercise, you were
supposed to enojarse con una persona sin culpa. And when
that person asked you why, you were not supposed to give
them any reason. Just "porque sí. PORQUE SÍ" And hopefully
it wouldn't come to blows, but if it did, you were supposed
to hold firm and go with it.

Marco--you know I'm not down with that.

I can send you the big conscientious objection that I wrote, my attempt to not just say fuck you, I'm not doing it, but respond with something artistic, and the art object I made which I thought again was beautiful and a little strange but the part you need to know is the response that I got in the taller. No one else had a problem with the exercise (although they almost all found ways to soften it, so they didn't really do what she asked). And when I said that I transformed, mediated the exercise, La Congelada unleashed her anger at me. She screamed at me. Told me that I had problems with anger. That I had a Pandora's box that I was afraid to unleash. "Aren't you ever angry? what about Martin Luther King! What about the fact that your ancestors experienced pain and your children might too just because of the color of their skin!"

"Of course, I get angry. But es injusto to inflict anger on someone who hasn't done anything to me. If performance art is not acting, then I don't understand how getting angry with someone who doesn't deserve it isn't acting." "Don't you see that every human being has done some kind of damage!" she shouted. "Maybe, but I don't think this is right," I said. "You think that art has to be good. Didn't we say that performance has no politics, no morality." "That was said in class, but no estoy de acuerdo." "Oh so you think that your little performance is going to change things . . . That is not what art is about! In a million years you could possibly change one person. You think you're such a good person." "Estoy tratando de ser una buena persona."

And then she turned it on. And she unleashed her anger at me. She called me names. Black. Fat. Ugly. She slapped me across the face two times. She kicked me. She took the writing that I'd brought about the exercise and ripped it into shreds. She took my art booklet and tore it into strips and threw it across the room. She tried her hardest to get me to buck, to scream, to unleash. And I wouldn't do it. I just stayed still and smiled and wouldn't respond.

And then I think I just checked out. I stayed very lucid and wouldn't allow any emotion. Because as you see, this

had turned into a war. And worse, a show. And I refused
to succumb to her manipulation. When she kept baiting me,
I kept responding what I thought. And at times, I would
speak in English until Myle (another one of those fucking
ay-ending names) said "No habla en inglés! No puedo
entenderte cuando hablas en inglés." And that for me was
the moment that almost made me crack because in the midst
of my beatdown, in the middle of class, the rest of those
mutherfuckers just sat there and let me get aggressed and
instead of saying or doing anything helpful, they want me to
respond to getting abused in fucking SPANISH just so they
can understand it all better.

Can you tell I'm angry now?!

Anyway, La Congelada dialed it down. Whatever she wanted
from me, she didn't quite get. And her whole story was like
"You think anger is violence. But I'm not asking you to be
violent. Nothing will happen if you do the exercise. You
*have* to do it. I know it's scary. You're in a different
country, you're a foreigner. But nothing will happen. People
will either walk away or think you're crazy. You're holding
on to your difference like it's some kind of refuge when
really you need to transcend. You need to go to that other
place. If not, no pasa nada con tu performance . . ." and on
and on. And then she kissed me on the lips and we went on
with class for another 20 minutes or so.

There's more to say about how the rest of that class went
and the looks full of pity that those other people gave me.
How I was sick when I came to class and how I felt worse
afterward but never lost my lucidity. How I went to the
Salon Corona right after and had tacos and beers with my
friends and actually met a small press poetry editor Andrès
Cisneros de la Cruz peddling books in the cantina. How I
felt like shit. Not that I hadn't fought back but because
as a black woman I felt and feel so much shame because I
let myself be abused in public like that--and I could only
imagine what my friends and family would say if they heard
about it. (Hit me once, shame on you. Hit me twice, shame on
me. Or Laurie Carlos telling my own performance class back
in MN, "I knocked that mutherfucker out!")

56

ME ENOJO CONTIGO

Agradesco infinitamente al Cristo del Veneno por darme la serenidad y fuerza de espiritu para resistir y soportar las agresiones que sufri por parte de "LA CONGELADA DE UVA" durante una sesion de su taller—"PENSAR PARA DEJAR DE PENSAR Y ACCIONAR" y ademas gracias a esta experiencia yo aprendi mucho del Arte del Performance y ademas acerca de mi misma.

OCTUBRE DE 2008
GABRIELLE CIVIL    MEXICO, D.F.

Clearly, I need to keep writing about all this. Phase one, the conscientious objection is written. And writing this to you right now is the body of phase two--my confrontation with the Congelada. Because it's really true: at one point, she said "tu no hiciste la acción." And I said, "Este es la acción." And I think that really was the exercise. But then there's phase three-which is the fact that I actually did do the exercise. I went to the Parque Mexico with my booklet and made a performance. I held the words "ME ENOJO CONTIGO" and for an hour put aside my beliefs and had encounters around "anger" and felt like shit doing it. And I need to write why I did it and about how the next day when I went to class expecting to be called on the carpet about doing it, she had completely let it go. And I had to tell her at the end of class--you know I did that exercise, although I did it in my own way. And we didn't even really talk about it. And the election was all wrapped up into it and I thought-- Why the fuck am I in Mexico right now? I should be with Martha & the Vandellas. Oh and the next exercise--required us to walk with stones in our shoes and I was walking on suckers and hard candies, making people angry when I wanted to be dancing in the streets . . .

And part of me really wants to quit. The taller. Mexico. Performance. But then I'm not a quitter. And as my pal Michael said to me in the United States of America, the ground of which I almost kissed when I arrived, "Gabby, I know there's raw emotion there. But this woman sounds like she's trying to take you to the next level. She's challenging you. And you're rarely challenged. So maybe something good is actually happening."

The teacher, the artist, the poet, the black woman are all grappling with this pinche taller. What's the education of an artist? What's the role of safety or terror? What's my relationship to anger? Should I embrace or release my grudge against all of them? What exactly am I learning? How can I not throw the baby out with the bath water. . .? So much of what I was working against had to do with that chicken bone necklace. How transgressive is the image of the angry black bitch? But maybe out of context, that isn't operating here . . . And you should see how warm the teacher is to me. When I skipped class on Monday, the note I received from La Congelada--"Gabrielle, mi reyna! Love ya . . . etc."

58

Anyway, writing to you has been helpful because I do
need to write this all down before it just turns into an
unproductive bad memory or just a chronic Haitian grudge
(and you know how we can be). I also need to figure out
how to bring back the spark to my own artmaking, use the
opportunities she's providing in the taller to do things
for myself, things that I might not normally do, but things
that can advance me as an artist without degrading me as a
person.

Today is the workshop. I have to get items from a specialty
shop and make a performance. I'll either use a hula hoop or
a plant that I'll then give to Daniel Hernandez as a late
birthday present. My heart isn't really in it right now. But
resilience is the heart of life. And right now that's the
work I'm here to do . . .

xo Abrazos Siempre,
Gabrielle

# ME ENOJO CONTIGO

A Performance—Objection—Meditation
*on a performance exercise by La Congelada de Uva*
Nov. 3, 2008


Get angry at someone who has done absolutely nothing
to you. You must not give them any excuse for your anger.
When they ask *por qué te enojas*, you respond *por que sí*.
¡ *POR QUE SÍ* ! You must not apologize. You must main
tain your ire. You must not return later and explain that
you really didn't mean it, that it's only an exercise for your
performance *taller*. It's not said explicitly that you must
provoke this other person, this unwitting partner, your victim.
But it seems like what you're really doing is picking a fight.
Isn't this what happens when you brush someone with
your anger. Doesn't it often come to blows? *Esperamos*
that it doesn't this time, but if it does come to blows
you must not back down. You won't like this exercise.
It will be hard for you and you won't want to do it.
What is unclear is what you will do, what exactly
will happen, who exactly you are where you are.

# ANGRY
# BLACK
# BITCH

In the *taller*, La Congelada tells us about an action
she did in the subway in Barcelona.
Holding on to the pole, she dropped her pants
down to her knees exposing her underwear.
No one blinked an eye.
In Mexico, she said,
this would have been transgression.
But in Barcelona, it wasn't enough.
And so, she came back with a full can of tuna,
which she ate in public on the subway car,
letting its stink waft throughout the train.
In Mexico, she said, no one would care.
But the Spaniards all turned up a nose.

**Performance, we discuss, is both deeply universal
and deeply culturally specific.**

Is this not the case both with anger and our bodies?

What does it mean for me as a black woman
performance artist to be unjustifiably angry,
potentially loud and verbally irrational in public?

In Detroit, in Greenwich Village, NYC, in Harlem,
in Minneapolis, in Paris, or the South of France
or other places where I've been . . . how would this play?

Would the folks there turn up a nose, shake their heads,
or would it even register as a blip on their radar?

# IN AND
# OUT OF
# PLACE

Would this exercise of anger

be like the necklace of chicken bones

I made for another exercise in the *taller*

which was meant to be disconcerting

but went far too well with my hair and skin . . .


To be angry (as a woman)

To be angry (as a black woman)

To be angry (as a black woman with a US passport)

To be angry (as an American)

To be angry (as a black American)

To be angry (as a black American woman in Mexico)

To be angry (                              in Mexico)

To be angry (                                        )


not as politics => as art as life as art


My friend Jennifer says:

"I don't get this—why does she want you to do this.

It seems like something out of an acting class."

But I know this is not about acting—

# KALI DESTROY ER

that in performance, even in an exercise,

whatever anger was generated would have to be real . . .


I also know La Congelada is smart,

a person and an artist to admire and respect.


In the *taller*, she pushes me, she pushes all of us

to go beyond our comfort zones, to become better artists . . .


That's why I wanted to work with her. That's why even though
I think this exercise is fucked up, that I can't imagine myself
actually doing it, I don't want to merely reject it, not do it, show
up empty handed. Yeah, yeah, the good girl hates not having her
homework done. But there's something else here that matters,
something to work through, figure out, come to grips with . . .
There's room to use this to become a better, clearer artist.

El enojo intones:

*I can provoke you*

*I don't fear my own anger*

*I am powerful and wily*

*I don't care if you like me*

*I don't care if you think I'm crazy*

*I can do whatever I need to as an artist*

*I can take the smudge on my soul,*

    *bear the psychic weight*

*I can put the world in its place*

*I don't have to be so damn nice all the time*

*I can bother you and annoy*

*I can unhinge myself with perfect control*

*I can take away your female squeamishness*

*I can be* la enojada, la perturbada, la loca,

  la mala chica, la otra sin reservaciones

# FRESA
# EXTRAN
# JERA

I think of my students saying about black
feminist lesbian mother warrior Audre Lorde:
yeah, she's alright, but why does she have to be so angry . . .

And I wonder: is my anger something
that I have not yet claimed?

Is it something I choke back?
Or avoid as feminine courtesy?
as a guest in foreign land?

Do I fear my anger will be endless
if unleashed like grief or loving the wrong man?

Or that I will just be seen as another crazy black bitch?
I get / have been / am angry at George W. Bush, the War
in Iraq, Carlos Slim, the customer service lady at Telmex
who was rude, cold weather, white people, Europe, snobs,
my Ipod for breaking, the crackers who tried to assassinate Barack,
the man who cut in front of me in line, back-stabbers and assholes,
sometimes my family, sometimes my friends, sometimes
myself . . .

# BALA PERDIDA

and I have swelled up with this anger, felt it fill me
like the cat who ate the canary or maybe even the tuna and
I have enjoyed it at times and congratulated myself on it . . .

**But my anger has always been specific,**
**and in my own mind, at least, for just cause.**

Me going off on someone in public who doesn't deserve it
reinforces pernicious stereotypes about black women as
difficult, capricious, negative, and unpleasant—stereotypes that
undermine real response to our real, justifiable anger.
Even if the context of this place is different, even if these
stereotypes may not be as prevalent or well-known here, they
loom large for me—as an artist and a person.

**Without cause, without justification, the source of my anger**
**becomes implicitly embedded in my body.**

(Oh the burden! the pleasure!)

# DRIVE-BY SHOOT ING

Even more than embodying or reinforcing stereotypes,

This exercise proposes another kind of violence and contributes

to the chronic baseless aggression already rampant everywhere.

Where I'm from, in this world, so much anger careening

without a clear source, a clear cause, already lands on the blameless.

Ntozake Shange says:

*"Ever since I realized there waz someone callt/*

*a colored girl an evil woman a bitch or a nag/*

*i been tryin not to be that & leave bitterness/*

*in somebody else's cup..."*

This exercise pushes me to think about the art

I want to make and the person I want to be.

Neither are neutral.

# GRINGA TURISTA ARTISTA

In his essay "Eureka!" Juan José Gurrola distills the essence of performance art and clarifies its difference from theater, from mimicry, from the morals and concerns of conventional society, conventional people and ideas. Performance art, he stresses, is not and should not be about politics or ethics or identity or culture. Intended as the perpetual vanguard of the avant-garde, it is poised to destroy all of these things.

We discuss this in the *taller*, the day of the anger assignment and I think:
That started off pretty good but,
what the fuck:                    I am a black feminist artist.
My politics, my ethics, my identity, my culture are all inextricable
from my body and my body of work.
These do not and should not offer my only readings.
But performance, like all art, like all action, is not
and never can be neutral: history, experience, context,
practice, circulation, and reception are all at play.
Not to mention energy.

Hasn't there already been enough destruction
of cultures, identity, ethics and politics?

I claim Gurrola's "Eureka" not as a new breach,
but as regeneration. Even or especially here,
I don't want to merely negate the negative.
The aim of my work is to open up space.

# OTRA LOCURA

I am searching, striving to make work that is intelligent, insightful, surprising, rich, warm, humorous, sassy, lovely, complex, challenging (for myself as well as for others), visionary, and honest.

**This work for me is deeply ethical**
**(again deeply universal and deeply culturally specific).**

I do not believe performance should be safe, easy,
flat, non-transgressive, or solely positive.
I just don't want my actions or my life to perpetuate
the same dirty tricks of the world.

And so, for this exercise, I offer three things: **conscientious objection, a mediation of words verbalized and sometimes written in bold, and this exchange:** my potential anger for that of La Congelada against me for my refusal of baseless anger, another kind of transgression, holding out for a transgression of kindness, other questions, more work, from *enojo* to *abrazos, otra locura,* baseless infliction of joy.

81

# An Intervention (Black Feminist Performance Art in Mexico)
## Selena La'Chelle Collazo

The significance of the intervention
The significance of the intervention of black
The significance of the intervention of feminist
The significance of the intervention of black feminist
The significance of the intervention of black feminist performance
The significance of the intervention of black feminist performance (art)
The significance of the intervention of black feminist performance (art) in Mexico
The significance of the intervention of black feminist performance (art) in Mexico City
The significance of the intervention of black feminist performance (art) in Mexico City
and new approaches to blackness in Mexico

Intervention in Mexico is a loaded word.

In Mexico City, the *Museo de las Intervenciones* features many interventions over the last five hundred plus years. What would it be like if, aside from the history of governmental takeovers, the museum included artistic interventions, interventions in the cultural conversation by people who refused to let the conversation play out without them?

*Los Estados Unidos de México* abolished slavery some fifty-five years before the United States of America. Mexico provided new hope for those who could escape enslavement by heading south, and special relationships formed between the communities of the Mexican northern states and the African Americans who made it there. This history, the connection to African enslavement, is spoken of in whispers and ghosts of memory in the repeatedly remade buildings and streets of the nation's capital. As such, which histories are inscribed upon Black feminist performance art in Mexico City? Which interventions are transferred?

How much of history is inscribed on our bodies, our performances, and our positioning?

At the time when Gabrielle Civil's performances took place, Mexico was preparing for its (bi)centennial. Children's textbooks were rewritten and museum exhibits were mounted to remind Mexicans about the role of Africans and their descendants in their country's history.

What does it mean to be an African American woman, triply marked as female, Black, and foreign, undergoing decidedly Black, feminist, performance art in this realm? How much of the U.S. context is imprinted upon her work? For the artist, is there an ownership of the work that is somehow more powerful when performed outside of the United States? Is the work read as foreign, and decidedly *estadounidense*, or is it hers, marked only by her body in conversation with the performance space, the specific performance site? How can this work relate to a renewed conversation about national identity? Is it possible for Black feminist performance art to permit a new self-reflection for Mexican audiences?

These questions are part of an ongoing conversation in which the marked body of the performer is inextricable from perceptions of the performance itself. This conversation is alive in both the performances of Gabrielle Civil and this book, which has a life reminiscent of, but distinct from, the performances (re)membered within. Her work, this book, the questions, and the conversation are all an intervention.

# Una intervención (Arte de Acción Afro-feminista en México)
## Selena La'Chelle Collazo
## traducido por Lucía Abolafia Cobo

El valor de la intervención
El valor de la intervención afro
El valor de la intervención feminista
El valor de la intervención afro-feminista
El valor de la intervención de una acción afro-feminista
El valor de la intervención del arte de acción afro-feminista
El valor de la intervención del arte de acción afro-feminista en México
El valor de la intervención del arte de acción afro-feminista en Ciudad de México
El valor de la intervención del arte de acción afro-feminista en Ciudad de México y nuevos enfoques sobre negritud en México

'Intervención' en México es una especie de palabra *tabú*.

En Ciudad de México, el *Museo de las Intervenciones* muestra muchas intervenciones a lo largo de los últimos quinientos años. ¿Cómo sería si, al margen de la historia de las tomas de poder gubernamentales, el museo recogiera intervenciones artísticas, propias de un diálogo cultural fruto de las gentes que rechazaron permitir la representación de tal diálogo sin ser tenidos en cuenta?

*Los Estados Unidos de México* abolieron la esclavitud unos cincuenta y cinco años antes que los Estados Unidos de América. México ofreció una nueva esperanza para aquellos que pudieron escapar de la tiranía llegando al sur del país, y un nuevo paradigma de relaciones especiales se formó entre las comunidades de los estados del norte de México y los afroamericanos allí asentados. Esta historia, la conexión con la esclavitud africana, nutre los rumores y los fantasmas de la memoria que albergan las calles y los edificios, continuamente reconstruidos, de la capital de la nación. De este modo, ¿qué historias se articulan en torno al arte de acción afro-feminista en Ciudad de México? ¿Qué intervenciones se transmiten?

¿Qué cantidad de historia está grabada en nuestros cuerpos, en nuestras puestas en escena, en nuestras posturas y puntos de vista? En el momento en el que los performances de Gabrielle Civil tuvieron lugar, México se preparaba para celebrar su (bi)centenario. Se reescribieron los libros de texto para escolares y las exposiciones de los museos se organizaron para recordar a los mexicanos el papel de los africanos y sus descendientes en la historia de su propio país.

¿Qué significa ser una mujer afroamericana, triplemente definida como mujer, negra y extranjera, experimentando un arte de acción decididamente afro y feminista, en este entorno? ¿Qué porción de contexto norteamericano deja huella en su trabajo? Para la artista, ¿existe una propiedad en su trabajo artístico que, en cierta manera, es más poderosa cuando se presenta fuera de los Estados Unidos? ¿Se puede interpretar su trabajo como una expresión extranjera, expresamente *estadounidense*, o representa ella misma, marcada tan sólo por su cuerpo en contacto con el espacio de acción, el propio lugar de la performance? ¿De qué modo se puede relacionar este tipo de arte con un diálogo renovado sobre la identidad nacional? ¿Le es posible al arte de acción afro-feminista ofrecer una nueva auto-reflexión a los públicos mexicanos?

Estas cuestiones forman parte de un debate actual en el que el cuerpo del *performer* no puede ser descifrado sólo con las percepciones de la acción artística en sí. Este debate está vivo tanto en las acciones poéticas de Gabrielle Civil como en este libro, un libro que da luz a una reminiscencia vital, aunque distinta de, los performances (re)cordados en su interior. El trabajo de Gabrielle, este libro, las preguntas y el diálogo, constituyen toda una intervención.

# DEAR RACHEL

11/21/08

Dear Rachel,

Yesterday, I had to bring an object which had strong
sentimental value for me to my performance art workshop.
Looking around my lovely, empty Mexico City apartment, there
wasn't much here with deep emotional history or resonance.
And I was also a little suspicious about what we would have
to do. Would I bring my gold hoop earrings that my mother
gave me for Christmas and which I wear everyday? Or would
I take a Xeroxed image of Maudelle Bass, which I love but
which could be easily replaced. How much could I afford to
risk?

In the end, I chose a black cloth angel which I bought about
fourteen or fifteen years ago. It's about palm-sized and
had cloth striped wings with small little black dots almost
shaped like hearts all over them. Everywhere I've gone,
that angel has been with me. New York. Minneapolis. Africa.
Spain. And now Mexico.

And so she came with me to class which began with my teacher
having us all look at the angel, smell it, feel it, touch
it, remember it. Then we all sat down in a circle on the
floor, and she pulled out scissors, a boxcutter, matches and
a bucket. "Gabrielle," she said, "tu vas a hacer una pieza
con tu objecto sentimental en que tu lo deshaces. [you're
going to do a piece with your object in which you *deshace*
it.]" "Deshacer?" I asked. "Es destruir [destroy]?" "Sí."

So I took a breath and cut the twine of my angel's wings.
And snipped off spare threads from her torso. And pulled off
her top and her little cotton pants. And I sliced open the
seam that connected her between her legs. And pulled out her
stuffing. And I turned her inside out. And twisted what was
left of her body and wadded it up by her head. And these
were all laid out in a row. And I thought I was done until
my teacher pulled over the bucket and the matches and we got

up and went to the patio and I took a match and struck it and watched a tiny little flame eat the wings and a bit of twine.

And before those flames went out, I took another match and lit up some of the stuffing. And finally, because the fire was so small, I took another match and laid it on her cheek and watched her face with its red stitched lips, and black stitched eyes and six small black knobs of stitches for hair dissolve in flame. And I watched it all with very close attention, not looking at anyone else. And of course, I was watching myself. And somehow this story speaks to everything we've been talking about and also what's going on for me in Mexico.

Love,
Gabrielle

# Algunas de sus acciones
# en la Ciudad de México
## Presentación en una galería de Motolinía, Centro
### por Sergio Peña

Dialoga con los espectadores, se ata las manos con varias cuerdas y cada una conecta con un espectador en particular. Ella está en el centro, como si fuera un corazón o alguien capturado, y al moverse, tanto espectadores como artistas oscilan de un lado a otro, unidos todos por las cuerdas, formando parte de un mismo ente, de un mismo tejido, literalmente: de un tejido humano. Y en esta ocasión, Gabrielle compartió escenario con varios grupos de performance, con propuestas muy diversas, siendo por ello evidente el resultado positivo de su presentación: se llevó la noche, los aplausos, la empatía, la energía y las sonrisas de un público que pudo atestiguar los excesos de algunos performances–por ejemplo, uno de ellos, que estuvo saturado de imágenes de mierda y gente comiéndola... Esa noche entendí que si hay un ingrediente que no puede faltar en las obras de Gabrielle, es la participación del público; es la otra mitad de la obra, las ruedas sobre las que corre, la carretera sobre la que circula...

# Selected Actions in Mexico City
## Presentation at a Gallery in Motolinía, Downtown
### by Sergio Peña
### Translated by Lucía Abolafia Cobo

She converses with the viewer. She ties her hands with several ropes—each one connects a specific viewer to another. She is in the center—resembling a heart or someone captured—and when she moves, the viewers and the artists oscillate from one side to the other, united by the ropes of belonging to the same entity made up of—literally—the same tissue: human tissue. This time, Gabrielle shared the stage with several performance art groups that had very different approaches, which made evident the positive result of her presentation: she took over the night, she received applauses, empathy, energy and smiles from an audience that was able to witness the excessiveness of some performances—one of them, for example, saturated with images of feces and people eating it...That night I understood that if there is an ingredient that can't be missing in Gabrielle's work, it's audience involvement. It's the other half of the artwork, the wheels on which it runs, the highway on which it moves.

# BRUSH

"Do you have good hair?" I ask at the door.
"Would you let me brush it?

"Sí, me gusta mi pelo," a young woman says.
*I do like my hair.*
"¿Por qué?" I ask her. *Why?*
As I brush,
she tells me her hair is pretty,
manageable, nice, good.
She had never really thought
about her hair before.
"I have good hair days and bad hair days,
but it's a part of myself.
Why wouldn't I like it?"
Why not, indeed?
*

"BRUSH" premiered at the final class recital of La Congelada de Uva's taller de performance "Dejar de Pensar y Accionar." I had made some intimate live art actions in class and one impromptu public exploration of anger, but "BRUSH" became my first official performance art work in Mexico City. By official, I mean it happened in a venue, featured other artists, attracted an audience who wanted to see performance art, and was publicized with a set date and time. I couldn't wait for the show!

The work itself came out of one of La Congelada's exercises.

"Write up a full application to present a performance action you have never done . . . Write out every gesture of your piece with as much detail as possible."

When she first gave these intructions, my mind blanked. Then I just started making shit up. Isn't that what artists do? I had come to explore being a black woman in Mexico, so why not start with something 101 like black hair? Black hair exists as a major cultural touchstone for African American women. Novels, songs, photographs, made-for-tv movies, the tradition is thick and long. Right now, off the top of my head, I can name: Benilde Little's *Good Hair*, bell hooks' *Happy to Be Nappy*, Ellen Gallagher's *DeLuxe*, Nikki Finney's "Tenderheaded," Solange's "Don't Touch My Hair," Octavia Spencer in *Self Made: The Madam C. J. Walker Story*, and Lonnice Brittenum Bonner's impressively titled *Good Hair: For Colored Girls Who've Considered Weaves When the Chemicals Became Too Ruff*. My favorite black hair work comes from my friend Rosamond S. King. It's called "the last poem I'll ever write about Black hair" and simply goes: "my hair is a tree/ and I must tend to it"

Writing my imaginary application, I started to see myself brushing my hair, started feeling the pressure of the strokes in my arm. The gesture of brushing held ambivalence and potential power. Was I trying to tend my hair or tame it? What if I could amplify that ambivalence and involve the audience? What if I could implicate them more directly in the action? In U.S. culture, the texture, the kinkiness, of black hair had been understood not just as ugly but unrefined and inferior. People with such hair were not seen as human: an idea which justified inhumane treatment towards them. Historical charts rank different hair textures, along with skin hues, head and nose sizes. Along with categorizing degress of humanness, these charts assert aesthetic values. The simple action of brushing my hair brought up racialized beauty standards, impossible self care, the pressure of hygiene and grooming, shame, and histories of racial violence. Before I knew it, the whole performance was down on paper, simple interactions with charged symbols.

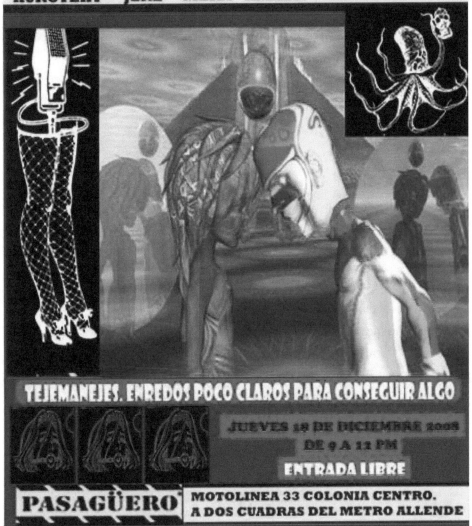

*

Presentación Colectiva de Dejar de Pensar y Accionar Taller
Jueves Diciembre 18 2008

Antes del performance, con el ayuda de otras personas,
buscamos y encontremos 5 personas para participar en el performance . . .
Ellos reciben instrucciones. . .

Bienvenidos a BRUSH
de Gabrielle Civil

Para participar en la pieza, tienes que cortar un poquito de tu pelo
de cualquier parte de tu cuerpo.
Dáselo a la artista cuando tú oigas la palabra BRUSH.
A cambio, tú vas a recibir un lazo.
Tú puedes llevar este lazo como pulsera o agárralo con tu mano.
Cuando tú oigas la palabra BEGIN,
tú tienes que mover tu cuerpo en todo el espacio en jalando y soltando el lazo.
Cuando el artista te señala directamente con el cepillo, deja el lazo.
Gracias por tu participación.

If you had asked me whether or not contemporary Mexican audiences carry different cultural associations, I would have said: of course, they do. Every day, things were happening all arond me that I didn't understand. Billboards, jokes, songs, historical references could all seem like koans. Even as I knew that my own grasp of Mexican cultural associations was limited, on some level, I still expected this audience to share my own.

With "BRUSH", I conceptualized a work with very specific cultural associations without considering how those associations circulated in this place or whether or not they even did. At the threshold of the performance, when I asked people arriving, "Do you have good hair?" many responded with blank stares. Some replied earnestly and politely without seeming to register the emotional weight of my question. What was loaded for me evanesced into passing conversation. This disconnect seemed more pronounced during the main action of the performance.

*

A hairbush hangs from a twine rope
encircled around my waist.
Five nooses also dangle from this rope
along with a pair of scissors.
Five volunteers from the audience first cut
a bit of hair from any part of their own bodies.
Then they pull hard on the nooses
to try and stop me from brushing my own hair.
Jazz plays in the background.
(Mingus, if memory serves.)
It's a battle: me, the brush, and my hair
versus specters of history
and the knowing/unknowing crowd.

*

For me, the image of the noose held violent connotations of lynching and racial violence. Watching YouTube videos to learn how to make noose knots had made bile rise in my throat. In the moment of the performance, the heaviness of the symbols seemed light. The volunteers slipped the nooses over their wrists and used the rope rings as handles. We push/pulled together across the floor in a new kind of weaving. One person in the audience told me later that the piece looked like a folkloric dance.

I loved making this work and showing it in Mexico City and it seemed like the audience enjoyed it. At the same time, I knew that the conceptual underpinnings of the performance probably hadn't come through. This was because, without realizing it, I'd been depending on the audience to fill in the context, the import of the symbols, the cultural associations all on their own. On some level, because I lived and breathed these ideas, I expected the audience to live and breathe them too. That's not a strong way to make performance art.

"BRUSH" alerted me to a lot of my bad habits. It's wrong to depend on embedded cultural signifiers or expect for an audience to just fill things in, especially an audience in a different place. It's also wrong to assume automatic responses to my black female body or specific notions of body itself. Of course, audience members in Mexico do have associations with race, gender, blackness, femaleness, American jazz, performance art, the body, and hair. This is true of audience members everywhere. What "BRUSH" helped me understand was that I didn't already know what those associations were. Moreover, for all of my black feminist scholarship and black femme lived experience, maybe I shouldn't be too sure of all the cultural associations and automatic responses back home either. Making work in Mexico City showed me that I would need to rethink things as a black feminist performance artist. Luckily, that was exactly what I had come to do.

# DOWN AND DELIRIOUS

The first time I talked to Daniel, he invited me over for a party. We met on a rooftop in Centro where expatriate journalists hung out, chewed the fat, and drank beer. What kind of stories about Mexico would they tell? How would their stories move across the wire? I got Daniel's contact from Daffodil, my friend Marco's serious girlfriend. She was a journalist, and Daniel was a journalist too. Slim and brown with dark hair, moustache and goatee, Daniel always had his ear to the ground.

Like Marco, Daniel grew up in California. He told me he purposefully didn't put an accent on his last name to mark his Chicano identity. He was raised in San Diego with deep ties to Tijuana but was fascinated with Mexico City. He had first come there to explore his roots. Now, he was writing a book about the contradictions of the city: ancient ruins and youth cultures, punk and emo, elite fashion parties, and neglected slums. His book ended up being called *Down and Delirious in Mexico City*. Daniel had stories to tell.

Over tacos and beer, we'd chat about current events, political scandals, the rise in deportation, the escalating drug war, Rihanna, a hip hop record shop he'd found, a new gay club, or a worker's strike. Journalism for Daniel was about being in conversation about many things and learning different sides of a story.

It was also about deeply being in a place. Before living in Mexico, I'd never met so many journalists before. Daniel. Alexis. Franc at *Al Jazeera*. Camilo. Jim. Margo, one of the few black women in Mexico that I knew. Margo and her husband Aran founded and ran *Inside Mexico*, a print monthly, from 2005-2009. When we met, they were trying to grow the magazine, maybe have it picked up by a larger company, but that never turned out. Instead, Margot ended up writing *Hidden Figures*, turning it into a movie, and hanging out with Pharrell. (Get it, girl!) Media has changed so much since those paper days. Now online is everything, and the local is not just global but digital/ virtual/ cyber social even AI media.

Things were still pretty analogue when I was living in Mexico. The first iPhone had only come out the year before. Facebook and Twitter seemed innocent. I had to learn to use T9 shortcuts on my flip phone just to text. Most people in my life didn't own smart phones yet. My camera was an actual device with film that needed to be developed. (I had to convince the guy at the photo place to print some naked photos of C. "¡Pero es arte!" I protested. "¿Ohhhh como Spencer Tunik?" he replied.) Pictures were on paper and so was a lot of the news.

I would walk past newsstands with Mexican tabloids hanging from hooks, their front pages blaring in silence. A body in a pool of blood with a slit throat. A person shot dead with the bullet shown nearby. A drug bust with a stockpile of guns. Those images jarred my expatriate bubble. *This place is more than just your magical art playground,* those newspapers said. *This place is serious, brutal, dangerous, intense, oppressed, unfair. Remember,* they reminded, *you're from Detroit, and Detroit can be anywhere.*

# AT THE HOTEL GÉNÈVE

It's election night, and I need French fries. The ones from McDonald's with a cheeseburger because what could be more American than that? Oh and snacks. I need snacks like Neo needs guns in *The Matrix*. Trans fats, sugar, and carbs. Secret weapons for coping. Hostess Twinkies, Doritos, peanut M&Ms, or as close as I can get: Bimbo Pingüinos, Taki Takis, or Krankys. I'm on edge in Mexico City. A real live Black Man is running to be President of the United States of America, and there's a chance that he could win!

Weeks earlier, I voted at the embassy, making my way through the armed barricade outside into a cool waiting room. There, a nice, white, Midwestern lady called my number and notarized my absentee ballot. Then, it was mailed back priority to the USA. At least that's what she told me would happen. I never saw it with my own eyes: I had to trust the system.

*(It's hard now to capture the early feeling.*
*For weeks, time and space blurred.)*

I know, I know, every era is historic. Every generation swears they lived through something momentous or magical. The violins swell and we dab our eyes and tell everyone far and wide how amazing/ hard/ unprecedented it all was. But damn! The 2008 election was really something. Back then, we thought George W. Bush was the worst politician imaginable, that 9/11 was the worst thing that could happen, and that the racist policies after Hurricane Katrina, or just being called racist in public, could be the worst political shame. Plus, the Great Recession was just jumping off, and more people were pissed off, broke, scared, and absolutely sick of the War in Iraq and the lies about Weapons of Mass Destruction.

It was time for a change. It was time for hope. That's the most amazing thing to me today. How many of us were *hopeful*, and how good it felt to hope and to believe that something better could happen. Today, hope for the future not only seems gone, it seems delusional (in the face of climate catastrophe and mutating viruses and the alt right and cancel culture and, and, and . . . )

Don't get me wrong. At first, we scoffed too. My friend Michael and I had a good laugh when Obama paid off all his parking tickets the day before announcing his candidacy. We liked his style. We liked that this

Black Man existed (and his wife really blew our minds). But we didn't take it seriously. We never thought he had chance. We never thought that he could shake up the system and get on the ticket. Then, he did it. *Don't Tell Mama, I'm voting for Obama* became a real thing. Hillary Rodham Clinton was out. Obama was in, and it was more than him. It was us. Turning out to vote, talking about grassroots community issues, bringing in new voters. Young people. Black and brown people. New Americans. The Somali woman in her scarf who walked in to caucus in Saint Paul, Minnesota with her baby in her arms and said, "OBAMA! Where can I write down his name?" She wasn't the only one. The country seemed alive, energized, mobilizing for something better. Glory! This looked to be the most exciting US election in my lifetime.

And I wasn't there. Living my glamorous life as a black feminist performance artist, I missed it. The entire last heat of the general election simmered without me. Indeed, I left for Mexico in August, before the Republican National Convention came to the Twin Cities. So many of my friends protested at the RNC. That's where my friend Marcus Young debuted the public dance practice Don't You Feel It Too? The RNC is what also brought my erstwhile lover Moe Lionel to town as a street medic to help protesters. (We would meet a couple years later when I was back from Mexico, restaging my "In & Out of Place" performances in Minneapolis. But that's another story.)

In Mexico City, at the time, some Fulbright expats remained active in Obama's campaign. Colleen Kinder was working with frequent flyer mile donations to help send volunteers to battleground districts. Other folks were fundraising. What was I doing? Other than sending a few nickels to Obama's campaign, my biggest contribution was discursive. I wanted to convince my relatives that he could win.

"Gabby, I'm sorry", my mother had said, "There's no way a Black Man will become President of the United States."

*"Mother, think positively!"* I chided. *"We have to believe!"*

It felt important to push for even the idea of the thing, a Black President. Even if I wasn't sure about Presidents, or about the nation, or the American political system, even if this person would never be perfect, I still wanted this to happen—on a symbolic level, on a deep cellular level—for some semblance of recognition or repair.

"Listen, it would be marvelous," my mother replied. "But you know where we live and I just don't think these other people can accept it. I don't want it to be true. But that's what I've seen all my life. I will vote for him but I don't expect him to win. But you know what, Gabby: *Prove Me Wrong."*

But what could I prove? Right or wrong, I'm watching it play out in Mexico City. George, Jennifer, and I have rented a hotel room to watch the election results on CNN. We aren't sure how things will turn out, so we want to be together. The Fulbright people recommended the Hotel Génève. Sumptuous, old world and a little kooky, it's touted as the "first establishment to serve a sandwich in Mexico." I'm hauling my bag of comfort food there. The fries are getting cold. My stomach is rumbling. My fingers are crossed.

Tonight we'll find out who wins.

January 15, 2009
Subject: knock on wood

Dear Marco--
Thank you for your kind e-mail. My mouth fairly watered when
I heard about the delicious soups you were making. Yummmmm.
It's been pretty chilly here and so I've been feenin' for
soup. Thought about making some (live right next door to
the marvelous Mercado Medallín) but have been too "busy"
e.g. lazy to do it. Have you always been such a cook? And is
Daffodil feeling better? Please send her my good wishes and
take some for yourself as well.

Which brings me to the Fulbright. Congratulations! The first
cut is the deepest and so it's wonderful news that you've
gotten through!

* * * * *

Since you've kindly sent your regrets for the art action
on Tuesday, I can tell you what's going to happen. With
the help and moral support of Daniel Hernandez, I went to
Garibaldi and hired a band of 8 mariachis to play and sing
for 30 minutes as close to the US Embassy as possible on
Inauguration Day . . . For me, it's a strong iteration of my
"In and Out of Place" concept and I think it will be fun to
see the DF workers listen to the mariachis singing a bunch
of black American songs in English on their lunch hour. I
plan to take lots of pictures and videos and will post on
FaceBook and other places. Whatya think?

All the drama with La Congelada continues to yield
interesting fruit. She's a good foil for me: thinner,
whiter, blonder . . . older, willfully apolitical . . .
hypersexual when I'm hyper cerebral. I suffered in the
taller, but I learned as well. I just have to figure out
what exactly . . .

I'm developing a performance called "Tie Air" based on the
experience--and presenting small pieces I made throughout
the taller to show in Minneapolis on March 13. My College is
flying me back to introduce Rita Dove at a College event (a
sure sign that there aren't enough black folks on faculty),

104

so I'm using the free trip to return and show some work. I
have high hopes for the piece and have already contacted
a pal in Puerto Rico about coming to his theater to show
it there in August. . . I think the process of writing and
performing will help me know more what I got from it all.

Okay pal--I'm in my pyjamas about to get underneath my
electric blanket. My pal Ira arrives tomorrow--coinciding
with the end of my 10-day cleanse. Tomorrow: tequila!

Abrazos,
tu prima,
Gabrielle

**Acción 20 de enero 2 PM / Art Action Jan. 20 2 PM**

P R E S E N T A N D O

**"In and Out of Place (MLK y Obama)"**

Una acción

de Gabrielle Civil

en Conmemoración de Martin Luther King, Jr.


y


en Celebración de la Inauguración de Barack Hussein Obama

como el Primer Presidente Negro de los Estados Unidos


Martes 20 de Enero a las 2 PM

en el Paseo de la Reforma cerca del Río Sena

(al otro lado de la Calle Génova)

En proximidad legal a la embajada de los Estados Unidos.

Esta acción durará aproximadamente 25 minutos

y es parte del proyecto Fulbright-García Robles

"In and Out of Place: Making Black Feminist Art in Mexico"


Todos Son Bienvenidos.


\* \* \* \* \*

# OBAMA, MARIACHIS & ME

I had a dream . . . that one day, on one of the most symbolic streets in Mexico City, I would sing and dance with mariachis for the inauguration of the first black President of the United States. We would sing soul songs, celebrating the occasion and commemorating the birthday of a Civil Rights pioneer. I would wear a special gown: a dark brown woman in bold, sparkly red. The mariachis would wear black.

On January 20, 2009, my dream, like the dreams of many around the world, came true. Barack Hussein Obama was inaugurated as the 44th President of the United States; and, on the corner of Paseo de la Reforma and Río Sena, a stone's throw away from the US Embassy—even closer to a political demonstration of shoes bidding farewell to George W. Bush—my art action "In & Out of Place (MLK & Obama)" occurred.

Before a mixed crowd of gringo acquaintances, local passersby and a surprising throng of photographers, 7 mariachis (3 violinists, 3 guitarists and 1 trumpeter) played: "Lift Ev'ry Voice & Sing" (the black national anthem); Stevie Wonder's "Happy Birthday" for MLK; James Brown's "Say it Loud (I'm Black and I'm Proud);" and Nina Simone's "Feeling Good." Although no Aretha Franklin, I sang, danced, held up pictures of my two honorees and tried to hype the crowd.

What does it mean for a Mexican mariachi to shout: "I'm Black and I'm Proud?" The older guys had given young Fernando Hernandez the sole responsibility of singing in English and he had all the lyrics taped to the back of his violin. I'm not sure he understood every word, but he certainly got their feeling. He announced, "It's an honor for us to be a part of this event. Obama's presidency speaks to the possibility of unity for all the races in the world." He spoke with fervor, but I'm not sure everyone heard his voice. I'm not sure what the rest of the crowd thought at all.

While one African American woman started to cry at the first notes of "Lift Ev'ry Voice," others had never heard the songs before or couldn't untangle the English. Some seemed quizzical, others removed. A few hurried by. More than a few just stood and watched, their cameras clicking and whirring. Not dancing, not singing, they took in the spectacle of me: in and out of place.

This art action allowed me to feel a part the inauguration festivities happening back home, but also marked my distance from them. As I danced and sang, I felt a strange mixture of solidarity and isolation, humor and homesickness, proximity and distance. This is the heart of my overall Fulbright-García Robles project: "In and Out of Place: Making Black Feminist Performance Art in Mexico." I am here to create, explore and share black art—in body and experience—in a different cultural context. It isn't always easy but is always worthwhile.

On that glorious day, it was my honor to play with those mariachis, to sing with my wobbly voice, to dance with pictures of those two amazing men, and to offer "In and Out of Place (MLK & Obama)" to a city which continues to challenge and inspire me as a black woman artist.

Gracias a San Judas Tadeo porque izo posible la
elección de Barack Hussein Obama como el
Presidente Nª 44 de los Estados Unidos de Norte-
america y para celebrar su elección y el cumpleaños de M.L.K. yo baile y cante con el Mariachi
en el Paseo de la Reforma cerca de la Embajada
Norteamericana. Gabrielle Civil. 24 de Enero 2009

# Mariachis à la Simone
# en Av. Paseo de la Reforma
## por Sergio Peña

Una canción de mariachi se escucha sobre avenida Paseo de la Reforma, la más importante de la Ciudad de México. La gente que camina por esta avenida se detiene a observar, atraída por el sonido del mariachi aunque algunos se sorprenden al darse cuenta que ésa no es una típica versión de música de mariachi, sino algo diferente, una interpretación bastante original, un mestizaje de la canción "Feeling Good", más conocida en la versión de Nina Simone; y suena muy bien en español, en la voz del mariachi que acompaña a Gabrielle, quien canta y baila sola, se mece, y contagia su entusiasmo a los que van pasando—y este evento tuvo lugar por los días en que se supo que el vencedor de las elecciones presidenciales en Estados Unidos había sido Barack Obama. Sí, un "Feeling Good" muy oportuno y contagioso, que activó la vida cotidiana de los habitantes de la Ciudad de México.

# Mariachis à la Simone
# on Paseo de la Reforma
## by Sergio Peña
## Translated by Lucía Abolafia Cobo

A Mariachi song can be heard on Paseo de la Reforma, the most important avenue of Mexico City. Drawn by the Mariachi sound, people walking along this avenue stop to observe. Some are surprised when they realize this is not your typical Mariachi song. It is something completely different—a quite original interpretation, a crossbreeding of the song "Feeling Good," best popularized by Nina Simone. And it sounds great in the voice of the Mariachi singing in Spanish accompanying Gabrielle, who is singing and dancing by herself, rocking and spreading her enthusiasm to those passing by. The event took place around the time when Barack Obama was announced as the winner of the presidential election in the United States. Indeed, a very timely and contagious "Feeling Good" that activated the daily lives of Mexico City's residents.

# In Mexico City
# Mariachis for Obama
## by Daniel Hernandez

Far from Washington, D.C., performance artist and writer Gabrielle Civil created her own homage to new U.S. President Barack Obama in Mexico City, on Tuesday, gathering mariachis to perform renditions of iconic African American songs both for Obama and the Martin Luther King Jr. holiday.

The art action titled "In and Out of Place (MLK y Obama)" happened just steps from the U.S. Embassy on Paseo de la Reforma and lasted less than half an hour. Mariachi Mexico Internacional, led by Señor Fernando Hernandez (a commuting immigrant to Atlanta) and his 26-year-old son Fernando, seen above leading vocals, sang four songs chosen by Civil. These were "Lift Ev'ry Voice and Sing," the Negro National Anthem, "Happy Birthday" by Stevie Wonder, "Say It Loud (I'm Black and I'm Proud)" by James Brown, and "Feeling Good," by Nina Simone.

Civil is a Fulbright fellow in Mexico City. She tells me: "The piece speaks to my feeling of being both 'in place' in Mexico, but 'out of place' here at a moment when an extraordinary thing is happening in my own country. [...] It has been a little bittersweet to miss such a historic election and inauguration. I grew up with generous, open optimistic parents who frankly told me there would never be a Black President in the United States ever. This art action is my way of being a part of the celebration, of sharing a little of who I am and how I feel with folks here."

Civil hired the mariachi a week in advance, handing them a CD and printed lyrics to allow the musicians to arrange and rehearse the songs according to the traditional mariachi style. So how "in and out of place" was it? A happy mix of musical dissonance and cultures colliding. The mariachi got into it. Pedestrians however observed the happening with meager interest; most people on busy Reforma went about their day as any other. The small gathering of U.S. ex-pats who showed up labored to chant "I'm black and I'm proud!" and not appear a little awkward doing it. See here and here for some footage.

Civil, in her case, clearly had a ball.

She says working in D.F. has been significantly impacting on her practice: "On my first visit to Mexico City two years ago, I was blown away by how differently my body circulated here, how the very arrival of my brown skin

114

and 'chino' hair could itself become a performance art event. [...] Mexico City is an extraordinary place full of culture, history, art and sophisticated thinkers from all walks of life. I feel blessed to be working here right now."

As for how the Obama presidency plays out in Mexico, Civil says, it's too early to say. "Mexico is a large, diverse country full of different people with different associations with the United States, African-Americans and African peoples from other places. Having a black U.S. president should have some impact on the way Mexicans and all people in the world view blacks—but we'll just have to wait and see."

# En Ciudad de México, Mariachis para Obama
## por Daniel Hernandez
## traducido por Lucía Abolafia Cobo

Lejos de Washington, DC, la artista de performance y escritora Gabrielle Civil realizó el martes pasado en Ciudad de México su propio homenaje al nuevo presidente de los EEUU, Barack Obama. Gabrielle congregó a varios mariachis para poner en escena su visión personal de canciones afroamericanas simbólicas, en honor a Obama y celebrando el Día de Martin Luther King Jr, fiesta nacional.

La pieza artística titulada "In and Out of Place (MLK y Obama)" — *Dentro y Fuera de Lugar (MLK y Obama)*" tuvo lugar tan sólo a unos pasos de la Embajada de EEUU en el Paseo de la Reforma y duró poco menos de media hora. El grupo Mariachi México Internacional, dirigido por Señor Fernando Hernández (un inmigrante que viaja a Atlanta cada día para ir al trabajo) y su hijo de 26 años Fernando, voces principales del conjunto, interpretaron cuatro canciones elegidas por Civil. Eran las siguientes: "Lift Ev'ry Voice and Sing", el Himno Nacional Negro, "Happy Birthday" de Stevie Wonder, "Say it Loud (I´m Black and I´m Proud)" de James Brown y "Feeling Good" de Nina Simone.

Civil está en Ciudad de México, acogida al Programa de Becas Fulbright. Como ella me dice: "El trabajo artístico que desarrollo trata de un sentimiento dual, el de sentirse 'dentro de lugar' en México y, al mismo tiempo, 'fuera de lugar' en este sitio y en un momento en el que algo extraordinario está sucediendo en mi propio país […]. Ha sido un poco agridulce perderme un periodo electoral y una toma de posesión tan históricos. Crecí y me eduqué con unos padres generosos, abiertos y optimistas que me decían, con toda franqueza, que los EEUU nunca tendrían un presidente negro. Esta acción poética es mi manera personal de sumarme a la celebración, de compartir con las gentes de aquí una pequeña parte de quién yo soy y de cómo me siento".

Civil contrató a los mariachis con una semana de antelación al acto, les proporcionó un CD y les imprimió las letras para que los músicos pudieran ensayar y adaptar las canciones al estilo tradicional de la música mariachi.

¿En qué consistió, por tanto, "in and out of place" "dentro y fuera de lugar"? Una mezcla lúdica y feliz de disonancias musicales, un encuentro de culturas. Los mariachis se involucraron completamente. Los transeúntes, no obstante, contemplaban el evento con escaso interés; la mayoría de la gente en el Paseo de la Reforma, como siempre tan concurrido, circulaba sin detenimiento y con prisa. Apareció un pequeño grupo de emigrantes norteamericanos que se esforzaron por cantar "I'm Black and I´m Proud!" sin parecer incómodos mientras lo hacían. Miraban aquí y allá, para salir en la grabación.

Civil, por su parte, claramente se lo pasó en grande.

Gabrielle explica que trabajar en D.F. ha sido notoriamente impactante para su práctica artística: "En mi primera visita a Ciudad de México hace dos años, me impresionó mucho cómo mi cuerpo circulaba de manera diferente por aquí, cómo la propia llegada a este lugar de mi piel negra y mi cabello 'chino', en sí mismos, podían suponer un acontecimiento artístico, un performance. Ciudad de México es un lugar extraordinario, lleno de cultura, historia, arte y pensadores sofisticados con tan variados estilos de vida. Siento que es como una bendición poder trabajar aquí en estos momentos".

Sobre el papel que jugará la presidencia de Obama con respecto a México, Civil responde que es aún pronto para saberlo. "México es un país grande y diverso, con una población muy heterogénea que mantiene múltiples tipos de lazos con los EEUU, los afroamericanos y los habitantes africanos de otros lugares. Tener un presidente negro en EE. UU. debería suscitar cierto impacto en la forma que los mexicanos y el resto de gente en el mundo ve a los negros—sólo tendremos que esperar y comprobarlo".

# FLASHBACKS

*¿ de dónde eres ?*

*where are you from?*

*and why are you wearing a sombrero?*

*are you trying to go native?*

*are you staking a claim?*

*are you playing a part or a joke?*

*who are you here, black girl?*

*who do you think you are?*

*what gifts are you bringing?*

*what rights do you have?*

*who are your people*

*and where are they now?*

*why is your accent so funny?*

*what are you trying to say?*

*when did you get here?*

*how long will you stay?*

*what lines are you drawing?*

*what are you rendering?*

*what do you recall?*

\*

I pulled the Fool again this morning.

Ever since returning to my Mexico book, this tarot card has been popping up a lot. Figures. Before smart phones with their portable global satellite positioning, I was the fool in Mexico, boundless and gleeful, getting lost with paper maps. I would ask everyone for directions: abuelas, children, street vendors, language teachers, taxi drivers, businessmen at taco stands, artists in museums. They served as my compass. I asked a million questions and they asked me some too. *¿De dónde eres?* always came first followed by *¿Te gusta México? ¡Claro qué sí!* I replied. *¡Me encanta!* Then, the conversation could veer off into myriad places before off I went— trying to find some other address, regain my bearings, meet up with new friends, or somehow make some art.

I actually bought my first tarot deck in Mexico City when I got off on the wrong Metrobus stop. Right in front of me stood a tienda de esotérica. Might as well go in. They were having a sale. I was having trouble with a performance. A gold Waite-Rider-Smith deck with a palm-sized guidebook in Spanish book beckoned me. They say you aren't supposed to buy your own tarot deck. They say a lot of things. But it was right there, I needed help, it called to me, I believed in it, a magical intersection of space and time, I was willing to go out on a limb. The World, The Sun, The Chariot, The Lovers, and yes, then and now, the Fool. All this in Mexico. Ooh, what a thrill! What a privilege, a struggle, an honor, an urgency for me to be there.

To some people, then and now, what a surprise.

*Mexico? I thought your family was Haitian . . .*

*Wait, wasn't your mother born in the South?*

Sometimes inheritance comes in different ways

or can move in surprising directions.

*

When Auntie died in Alabama, she left some money to my mother, and so my parents took a trip to Mexico. AAA planned it all out: Acapulco, the silver city of Taxco, Cuernavaca, and the capital, Mexico City, where the high-speed underground metro was still pretty new. This was 1977. They were there when Elvis Presley died. My father is fluent in Spanish, so the language barrier didn't have to apply. They visited murals, shopped in markets, and danced in nightclubs. My mother got pickpocketed and suffered Montezuma's Revenge. This didn't stop them. It was part of the adventure, par for the course. They saw the sights and bought souvenirs. I flipped through their pocket guide to Aztec archeology and slipped my mother's chunky Mexican bracelets over my wrists.

"I can't believe you all didn't take that money and invest it," I recently teased, "or put it in a college fund or wait to take us with you. You all just hit the road!"

"Wasn't that the right thing to do?"
my mother asked without remorse.
"Absolutely," I agreed. *¡Claro que sí!*
They didn't talk a lot about that trip in my childhood
(too busy working themselves to the bone),
but the evidence was all around our home.
My parents weren't just *from* places, they had *gone* places.
For pleasure and edification and because they could.
What a trip! What wonderful footsteps to follow . . .

\*

Too often, as a black woman, my geography has arrived already circumscribed: captivity and slave routes, Harriet Jacobs in her grandmother's attic, Harriet Tubman with her do-rag derring-do, the Underground Railroad, the Great Migration, stories of porters on trains safeguarding grandbabies, going to Boston in a game of Bid Whist, road trips down south (with fried chicken and sandwiches packed in the back because the diners wouldn't serve you), family reunions, *Roots* (which I never saw), diaspora loss, slave castles, Black to Africa, freedom marches, Rosa Parks sitting in the front of the bus, my father's flight from Port-au-Prince, bulging suitcases on his summer trips back home, yellow cardboard cases of Rhum Barbancourt from the airport, Haitian cousins sitting all day at INS for green cards, brain drain, scholarships, and the Kingdom of Detroit. I receive and claim all this inheritance as mine.

Still, I wanted more.
Where was wandering,
witnessing, broadening horizons?
Actually not knowing the way?
Maybe it was foolish,
*(I was willing to go out on a limb)*

121

but I sensed something else out there
off the beaten path
another archeology,
an unexpected bequest,
my body translating, shifting
across and between borders . . .
freedom, pleasure, and delight,
an expanding trajectory—

\*

I was looking for new passages, and as always, books spurred me on. After racing through *I Wonder as I Wander* by Langston Hughes, I went on a trek for black women's travel narratives. In libraries, I stumbled onto *Wonderful Adventures* by Mary Seacole, *A Long Way from St. Louie* by Colleen J. McElroy, *Russian Journal* by Andrea Lee (her first book *Sarah Phillips* starts in Paris and the black people could swim!), *Black Girl in Paris* by Shay Youngblood, *Museum* by Rita Dove, *The Heart of a Woman* by Maya Angelou, and a trip to Mexico (*¡Ándale!*) deep in the middle of *Zami* by Audre Lorde. My parents had brought home souvenirs. These books became an archive. Here was hunger and glamour, curiosity and surprise, foibles and error, intimacy and distance far from expected confines. Here were black women artists on the move, traveling on and off the page.

\*

Travel has been central to my personal and creative growth. I studied abroad in France, my Junior year in College (*Why aren't you going to Africa?* my aunt Mary grumbled) and traveled around Europe on a Eurail pass. I spent time in Haiti visiting relatives, performing, and taking part in a post-earthquake grassroots relief effort. I've visited Morocco and Iceland (in both winter and summer). I've also performed in many places: Canada, Puerto Rico, the Dominican Republic, Ghana, The Gambia, and Zimbabwe. Making art in a place offers a different way to be there. It doesn't mean that you're still not a tourist, a traveler, a visitor, but you also have to be something else: a witness, a contributor, a collaborator with the people and the place. Every day in Mexico, people questioned me about my presence and origin. (*¿De dónde eres?*) Every day I had to respond and question myself and those around me. Without direct, ancestral lines to this place, without a clear role in the national story, I got to live the intersection of nationality

122

and race differently. Like all expatriates, I had to examine my relationship to my own home country and the privileges of my US passport. I got to think expansively about disconnection, diaspora, and relationality. I had to confront my own essential assumptions and recall nagging expectations.

*

*Why aren't you going to Africa?*
my aunt Mary grumbled.
Well, my school didn't have
a scholarship for that.
I do want to go to Africa.
I will go. I did go
and want to go again.
At the same time,
ancestral return
weighs heavy
with expectation.
Standing in the
Door of No Return
on Gorée Island
I am expected
by my aunt Mary
by tour guides
by cultural agencies
by locals who feel
sorry for me
by people at home
who feel proud
who feel wistful
who feel lost
who feel hopeful

to feel a certain way.
But what if I don't?
I encounter circling back
as a demanding precedent
and pressure of feeling.
But when circling around
a massive pre-Columbian
African head in Veracruz,
no one expects me to be there.
Or at the ruins in Tulum
or Teotihuacan or the urban
monument of El Ángel.
How do these shifts
in location inform
my sense of diasporic
blackness in the world
and in myself?
In Mexico,
the expected
response
was unclear
making me feel
more free to feel.

*

I first went to Mexico City in 2007 and then lived there from August 2008 through December 2009. For over fifteen years, I've been trying to circulate my performance/writing from that place and time. Now consider how much the world has changed.

(Also how much it hasn't.)

How to talk about world travel today?

It is 2024, and the world is still grappling with the impact of the Covid-19 global pandemic. The coronavirus has mutated through Delta and Omicron variants with more strains on the horizon. Just this January, I got Covid for the second time even after being vaccinated and receiving multiple booster shots. Covid, downgraded to an endemic illness, can still wreak havoc in our lives. It can still wreck our plans, snatch our money, ravage our bodies, infect our friends, lay us up in bed, and leave us stuck at home. Or at least, that's what just happened to me. The world is open and we can always wear masks. But what kind of public gathering is worth the risk? For sure, some people, have never missed a step, have ridden shotgun, or flown business class through the worst of the public health crisis, but for many people just stepping outside remains a fraught or punishing proposition.

And travel to another country, for pleasure and edification? Just because you can? In some circles, the carbon footprint of taking an airplane already constitutes a sin. (*What are you doing, black girl? The polar ice caps are melting! Are you trying to destroy the planet!?*) While the world is always rotating, the current level of global political instability is profound. A short list would include the genocide in Gaza, the war in Ukraine, profound conflict in Haiti, Congo, Sudan, and Armenia, and a border crisis in the U.S. that includes a vicious campaign against migrants by a hyper-xenophobic alt-right. On the other end of the spectrum, words like *explorer*, *adventurer*, and *tourist* can vibrate like *settler*, *colonizer*, *imperialist*, and *capitalist pig*. With these dynamics, endorsing travel can make you sound like a fool at best, tone deaf, or morally corrupt at worst. Or maybe travel is palatable as long as you stay in your lane even while away.

My friend Allison told me about some friends in Senegal who run a study abroad program in Dakar. They report that students (by that, I mean predominantly white students) don't want to wear wax clothes at Senegalese formal events out of fear of appropriation. Those clothes don't belong to us, they think: it would be wrong for us to wear them. In the meantime, what t-shirts, Carhartts, or other sloppy duds are they sporting at posh affairs? These students don't want to be culturally disrespectful, but, for the host families, wearing wax is a way to show respect for the culture. Showing up not wearing the appropriate wax clothes can become the disrespectful thing. Students will wear cheap tourist bracelets (with no ingrained cultural value) but will refuse resplendent garb tailored just for them. (Wax fabric is originally Dutch, making this rejection especially rich.) Host families shake their heads.

What makes the students so sure that their US idea of appropriation is shared around the globe? Or that the terms are the same in the new place? How does appropriation relate—or differ from—cultural participation? Are the wax clothes, tailored specifically to the wearer's body, just too beautiful for shame-ridden, anxious Americans to wear? Do the students only deserve cheap tourist bracelets? And if that's the case, why are they there? What did they come to do? Are you allowed to go to a place but only go so far?

As we reckon with historical harm, it can be hard to imagine any cross-cultural encounter beyond domination and oppression, exoticization, or consumption. And certainly, in Mexico, there's justifiable suspicion of gringos with smug buying power crossing the border for cheap prescription drugs and partying as los spring breakers in Cancún. Yet, as the child of two people from two different countries and cultures, one of whom is an immigrant, I know more options exist. As a black feminist performance artist, my job is to imagine and figure out possibilities, experiment, and embody new forms of being.

*

We need more models and honest conversations about making art in other places. We've seen some *bad* examples (yes, Gauguin, I'm talking about you), but the artist in another place doesn't have to be a predator. She shouldn't think of herself as a savior or a default public servant either. Even or maybe especially, if the work is public, it's key to understand that your presence is just one tiny element in the ecosystem of the place. (As Kendrick says, "Be humble. Sit down.") You might be making a public performance art work, for example walking with candy in your shoe in a public park, navigating personal dynamics of anger and shame. As you're doing your black feminist performance art thing, maybe people shake their heads or cock their heads to the side and look closer or roll their eyes or take a glimpse and then turn back to more important matters. Maybe they stare or walk up to you and ask questions. Maybe they don't even register you at all. Making art in another country might lead to a transformational cross-cultural exchange and maybe it won't be that deep, at least to the people in the other place. Just the same as at home, the key thing is to do your work and do your best not to be an asshole.

*

None of this is automatic or easy. Questions of intention and territory, exploitation and heritage are always on my mind. (Yes, I've rolled my eyes at white girls wearing African braids on the beach.) Yet, rigid ideas about cultural ownership seem more about external perceptions than actual encounters with local people. What do they want? How much do they even care about our lofty plans? How much are we still tuned in to U.S.-based opinions or Facebook screeds? I'm not in Senegal with the students and host families, so I can't judge what's happening there. Except of course, many people do judge from afar. With this Mexico book, I am aware that some people may judge me.

> *(why are you wearing*
> *a sombrero, black girl?*
> *who do you think you are?)*

*

I see a close-up of myself on a long scroll of white paper wearing a sombrero.
Does it matter that this photograph was taken at a live performance?
Does it matter that the sombrero was something that I bought for myself?
Does it matter that my friends in Mexico City told me where to buy it?
Does it matter that it came from a small place where they sometimes
    bought gifts?
Does it matter that I joked with the vendor who sold me the sombrero?
Does it matter that I didn't bargain for the price? Or at least not very much—
    just enough not to seem like a stupid gringa,
    but not so much as to be rude . . .
Does it matter that I collaborated with mariachis on performances?
Does it matter that I loved them?
Does it matter that I don't really know how they felt about me?
Does it matter that they were always kind and professional?
Does it matter that the sombrero served as an emblem of them for me?
Does it matter that almost a decade after my parents traveled to Mexico,
    my mother started working in Southwest Detroit?

Does it matter that Southwest Detroit is predominantly Mexican?
Does it matter that they struggled at first to understand each other,
   the African American lady principal and the Mexican American families?
Does it matter that they came to love each other?
Does it matter that it took time?
Does it matter that on her last day of school before she retired,
   they surprised my mother with an assembly
   where mariachis came to play?
Does it matter that my mother was honored
   and delighted by those mariachis?
Does it matter that this sombrero becomes an emblem
   of those mariachis too?
Does it matter that all these memories synthesize?
Does it matter that multiple performances are not collapsing
   into each other but existing together all at once?

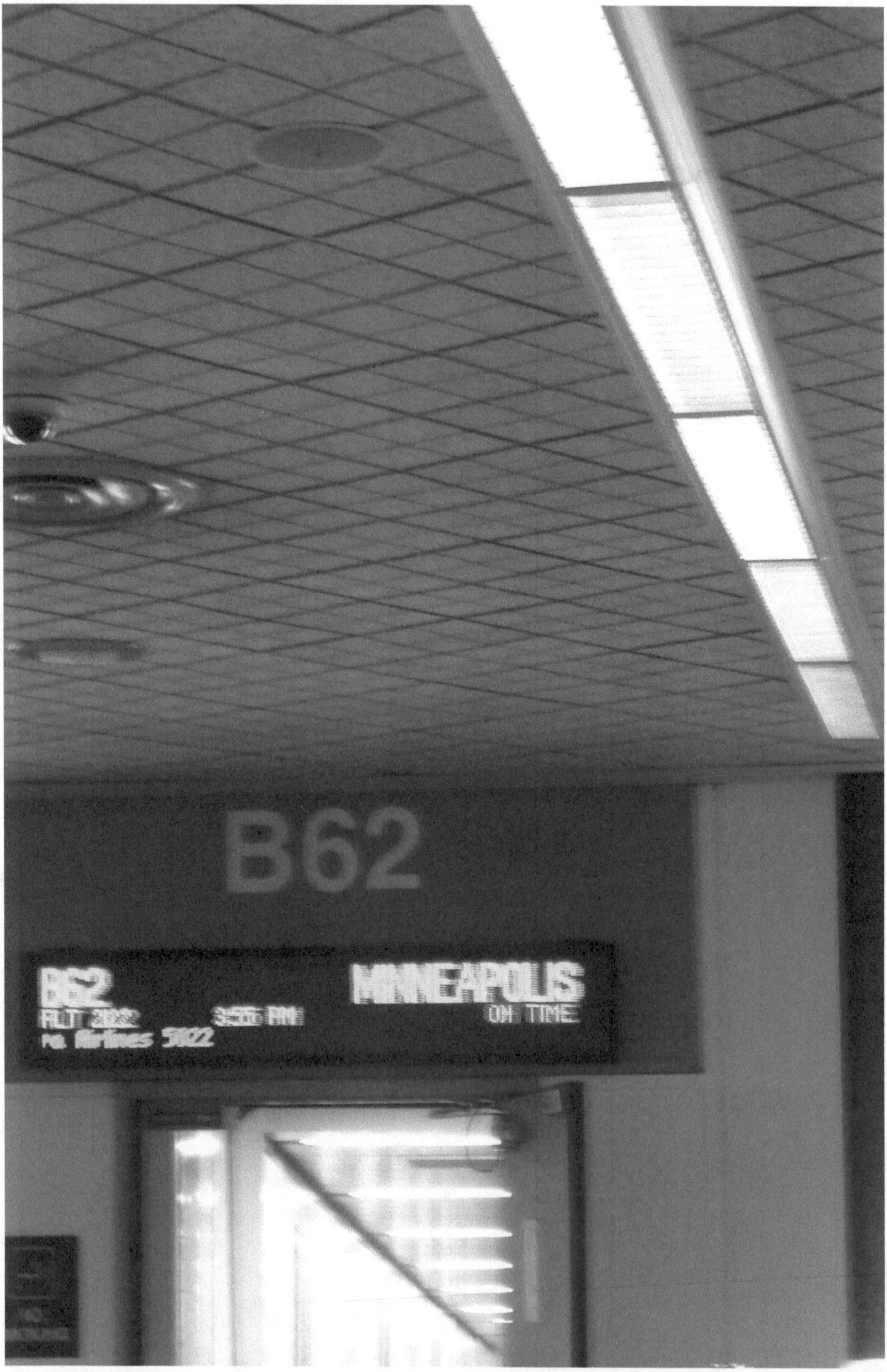
B62
B62
MINNEAPOLIS
ON TIME

"On some level I felt obliged to make art.
Beyond that attempt is the truth of trying
to understand something other
than what I have known."


"Hasta cierto punto, me sentí obligado a hacer arte.
Más allá de esa tentativa, se esconde la verdad
de intentar comprender algo más
de lo que ya sé."


—Ralph Lemon

# TIE AIR

So I give you this sun,
diamond dense, diamond hard,
so strong it's turning
everything bright, everything dark
and darker. You touch
your face, your chin and wonder
am I growing hair?
am I turning to velvet?

*

How to account for transformation? An enduring problem for me has been conveying what happened in my life in Mexico. On the one hand, I arrived as myself in my own language and my own body. On the other hand, amazing things started happening in language and body, so that I was myself but also someone new. What happens to that new person upon return? Black diasporic literature tackles this age-old question, especially in narratives of education. People in a black community, a colonial state or ghetto, want the scholarship boy (or more rarely girl) to go off, get an education, and come back to help uplift everyone else. Trouble arises when the newly educated person comes home. Not only can't he/she/they seem to translate or transfer what happened, but now they/he/she seem like someone else. This can be profoundly alarming. (Just ask Aimé Césaire in *Notebook of a Return to My Native Land*, Samba Diallo in *The Ambiguous Adventure*, or Bita Plant in Claude McKay's *Banana Bottom*.)

How to apply learning from another place?

My performance *Tie Air* showcased my experience in La Congelada de Uva's performance art workshop (or *taller*) in Mexico City. Taking place in the now defunct Center for Independent Artists in Minneapolis, *Tie Air* is the only performance art work from my Fulbright project "In and Out of Place" to premiere outside of Mexico. I'd left in Minnesota in August and hadn't been back in over six months. I wanted to share some of what I'd learned and show a little of what I'd become. I wanted to bring my Mexico into Minnesota.

# TIE AIR
*(from my notebooks)*
## a showing of new performance work
*hecho en México*

by Gabrielle Civil Center for Independent Artists Friday March 13 2009  8 PM
Today's Worksheet: Thurs. March 12, 2009 (Happy Birthday Eric Leigh!)

Original Concept: To show performance art work generated in the *taller* or workshop
that I took with Rocío Boliver aka La Congelada de Uva in Mexico City from Oct-Dec.
2008.

Developed Concept: trifold
  —show short pieces made from the taller
  —comment on / transform the experience of the taller
  —overall create an /abstracted/ aesthetic experience from my experience
      so far as a black feminist performance artist in Mexico

Influences / Things I'm Thinking About Now:
the tension between <u>knowing and not knowing</u>; being deemed too abstract and
obtuse vs. overemoting, being over explanatory; action and gesture vs. narrative
and explanation; the power of chance;  Mexico vs. \Minnesota (In and Out of Place);
Marina Abramović' "Mambo," Tamatz Juanes' *pavo navideño*; what I most learned in
La Congelada's taller

Source Material:
Piezas / events from el taller con La Congelada de Uva + Me Enojo Contigo art book
& interview *ice - chicken bones – esperanto - still life – transgression – <u>anger</u> - applauso  -
candy <u>angel sacrifice</u> - artist report – dice – stick- lick- purple rain- black magic- solicitud-
brush* +  L. letter

Things I'm thinking about: sexual encounters; engaging / resisting anger, my life in
Mexico; my challenges & growth as an artist; fear of returning to Minnesota; dealing
w/ various kinds of cold…

Images/ Elements: hands trying to tie air, L. and me Mexican /French /kissing; ice
(what I crave, what I dread and also a link to La Congelada herself!); candy; hard
sweetness; dancing with pain; pouring out; throwing dice; staying on my toes;
dealing with cold

Signature aspects:
thresholds, language, mix of reading and reciting, projections, movement
Element to play with again: Josina or another tech person as a kind of interlocutor?
Playing with: tightness and looseness—set points and what can happen in between
Balance: the need for clarity and foreknowledge of actions with the idea of *play* and
*spontaneity*

There was too much material. I wanted to recreate some of La Congelada's performance exercises but also highlight something about race, anger, and desire. I had a bunch of short videos: *Here Come the Whites*, a tiny riff on minstrelsy; a video of me interviewing a Mexican stranger about anger from my project "Me Enojo Contigo;" a video of me burning my angel in La Congelada's taller; a video of me French kissing L. (I loved the play of "French" kissing in Mexico); and a video of my hands "tying air." On top of that, it felt crucial to contrast the sweetness and warmth of Mexico with the coldness of Minnesota, so I was interested in candy and ice. Images and ideas accumulated until I landed in town without being sure of what exactly the show would be.

*

Back in Minnesota, I was struck by how familiar and unfamiliar things were. It was very cold and very white, it felt very close and very far away. By then, I'd lived in Minnesota for over seven years, had struggled with loneliness and also built a kickass artist community. I'd felt very double there, and when I got back, I could feel my previous disembodiment floating in the air, a clamoring twin, trying to land back on my skin. This performance could help me combat that dynamic and enter into a new phase.

A few days before the show, I was still figuring out the order of the performance actions when my friend Molly gave me a brilliant suggestion: let the audience decide what you'll do. This felt right because it allowed me to cast a broad net of possibility and relinquish some control. These had been important gestures for me in Mexico. In La Congelada's taller, I'd done a short piece using dice, a rare work of mine that she liked. I stood holding and shaking dice for three minutes to magnify both the inertia and the possibilities of chance. This resonated with *Tie Air*, so I decided to number a series of performance actions from one to twelve and then ask an audience member to throw the dice. I would do the action of that corresponding number. Actions came straight from my notes about the taller and included:

Do a simple action for three minutes.

Have others watch you.

Alter your body in a way that is subtle but unsettling in public.

Walk across the room without walking.

Tell your life story in a language that doesn't exist.

Do something transgressive in public.

Make a performance using your bodily fluids.

Tell a story from your childhood for three minutes

the way you would tell it as a child.

You must do this completely naked.

Create an *estampa congelada*, a tableau vivant

in which you will be the center.

Decide on one specific gesture.

Repeat this gesture in set rhythm over time.

Chance performance actions would be interspersed with pre-set actions and select videos. It would end with me activating my body with candy and ice while Prince's "Purple Rain" (a Minnesota classic!) played in the background.

   To initiate travel and chance, audience members had to throw dice when they arrived at the box office. They were given a piece of candy to put in their shoe. Then they would walk to the theater pausing after however many number of steps they'd thrown with the dice. (This riffed on the taller exercise: "Walk 150 steps away . . . Make a performance from something you find there.") When they arrived in the theater, I was already dancing with hard candy in my shoes. The audience was invited to join me dancing but, this being Minnesota, no one really did, and I didn't really expect that they would. Once everyone arrived, I stepped out of my shoes and poured a torrent of candy from inside them all over the stage.

   What sweet, secret pain resides in our steps?

   Making performance art can be hard and sweet.

   I'm usually fastidious about performance documentation (forever haunted by all the lost work of Maudelle Bass and Anne Spencer and other black women artists). For some reason though, most images and video of *Tie Air* have disappeared. Only notes, memory, and feeling remain. Doing *Tie Air* felt surreal like colliding worlds, a blur of image, action, and sensation. Sucking ice for three minutes, I remember the cold on my tongue, the predominantly white gaze of the audience, my suffering at how long three minutes can take, my marveling that I had lived in Minnesota for so much longer.

# TIE AIR

Notes for Friday March 13, 2009
Gabrielle Civil – Josina Manu (tech) – Sarah Stockholm (stage assistant)


THRESHOLD
            *dice*
*pasillo*                    *candy trail*

CANDY SHOE            - - ->        dancing with pain

*from da church to da palace -> candy spill   candy clearing*

                *dice?* [here or wait?]

                [??? Tie Air Eyes Video???]

*Bienvenidos*        / TMI!   / *welcome to the show*        <u>w/ Josina translation</u>

                Tie Air Kiss Video

        *Drag in the bag of ice*

            *Eat it . . . .*

                [??? Tie Air Eyes Video???] or [Angel Sacrifice Video?]

DICE THROW / EJERCICIOS     [hand out cards with the exercise list and numbers]

throw the dice three times and do whichever three exercises

Tie Air Hands video?                    *End with my body tying air ?*

        ME ENOJO CONTIGO

            Me Enojo Contigo Video

                *[La Congelada's response with paper mask]*
                Work with the ice . . . .
                Have everyone place a piece of ice on my body
                    [douse me with the icy water]
                    [voice over of my childhood story---]
                    *the sounds of Purple Rain . . .*

Working Script (Evolving)
t h r e s h o l d

*dice*                 people arrive; throw dice and pay what lands
                       receive candy and directive: they must
                       put at least one piece in one of their shoes

*pasillo*              they walk down the hallway which has a glittering trail of candy
                       they feel their own candy underfoot
                       they hear amplified loud music—it has already begun

*candyshoe*            they walk through the backdoor into the theater space
                       I am already dancing with candy in my shoes
                       at moments they see me stop and add more and keep dancing
                       they are invited to dance with me
                       a crepe paper cord stretches across the seats:
                       they are not allowed yet to sit
                       there is dancing with pain          they are in it
                       they can join in or watch
                       this happens for a while
                       at a certain point—the crepe paper gets moved away and people can sit
                       at a certain point the lights dim, the music fades out
                       a spotlight grows on my action in the space

*estampa*
*congelada*            for a few minutes, I become very still—
                       develop the gesture which is taking off the shoes
                       pouring out the candy
                       filling the shoes with candy
                       putting them on
                       taking off the shoes
                       pouring out the candy
                       slowly and in rhythm
                       and they are sitting and watching
                       this happens for a while
                       the lights fade to black

                       SHOW!
*clearing the*
*space*                I get on my hands and knees and push away the candy
                       give myself space to work
                       push the sweetness to the edges
                       and land back on something bare

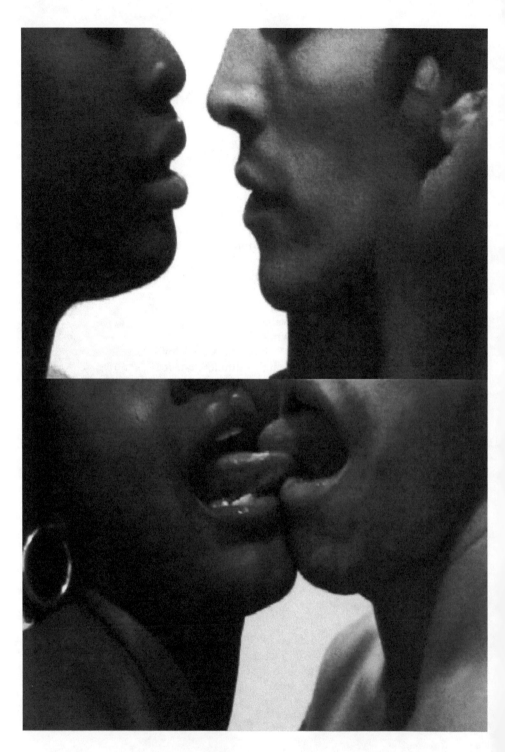

# On "Tie Air"
## Juma B. Essie

Sweet hobbling.

"I know where this is going," I thought as Gabrielle instructed us to put
the piece of candy in our shoe and make our way into the theater. Walking
uncomfortably down the hall, I ran down the list in my head: subject verb agreement,
le or la, should I put down my knife after cutting, are my shoes too neon. The
impediments of traveling, that's what I was expecting. But, I was soon surprised and
caused to question my own perceptions and expectations. They broke down—

The impediments of traveling as a US citizen

The impediments of traveling as a Black American

The impediments of traveling as a Black American woman

The impediments of traveling as a Black American woman artist

Now embody them all. Here is Gabrielle, sexy beautiful, kissing a man. Large on the
screen. Seeing and being seen like some mead show and tell. The line between the
audience and the artist is either named some sort of voyeurism or some sort of embodied
feeling. It is usually defined by the quality of the artist's presence. Gabrielle's presence
made it clear that observation without participation would be impossible. When she
talked about her experience in a performance workshop I was with her. I felt the sweet
hobbling of navigating language, culture, and artistic integrity. And when she stood
present and silent melting ice in her hands I also feel the cold that becomes heat, the
sweet hobbling of giving over to being present and feeling in one's life.

140

# Acerca de "Tie Air" / "Atar el aire"
## por Juma B. Essie
## traducido por Lucía Abolafia Cobo

Un leve cojeo. Un sufrimiento leve.

"Sé dónde va todo esto", pensé mientras Gabrielle nos ordenaba ponernos el caramelo dentro del zapato y dirigirnos hacia el teatro. Cuando bajábamos, incómodos, hasta la sala, repasé la lista en mi cabeza: concordancia entre sujeto y verbo, le o la, debo soltar mi cuchillo después de cortar o si el neón de mis zapatos es demasiado intenso. Los obstáculos del viaje, eso es lo que estaba esperando. Sin embargo, pronto llegó la sorpresa y esto me provocó cuestionarme mis propias percepciones y expectativas. Todas se desvanecieron—

Los obstáculos del viaje siendo ciudadana de los EE. UU.

Los obstáculos del viaje siendo una americana negra

Los obstáculos del viaje siendo una mujer americana negra

Los obstáculos del viaje siendo una mujer artista americana negra

En este momento los encarno todos. Aquí está Gabrielle, tan sexy y hermosa, besando a un hombre. Se le ve grande en escena. Nos mira y la miramos como si fuera licor de miel; nos enseña y nos cuenta. Se podría determinar la línea divisoria entre el público y la artista como un tipo de voyerismo o como un sentimiento personificado. Normalmente se define por las cualidades que despierta la presencia de la artista. La presencia de Gabrielle nos deja claro que la observación sería imposible sin participación. Cuando nos transmitía su experiencia en un taller/performance, yo coincidía con su postura. Sentí el dulce sufrimiento de una lengua, una cultura y una integridad artística que son nómadas. Y cuando se quedó quieta, tan presente y en silencio, derritiendo hielo en sus manos, también yo sentí el frío que se vuelve calor, la tenue dolencia de renunciar para estar presente y sentirse vivo.

# << M N – M X >>

At one point in *Tie Air*, a genial white man in the audience threw the dice. The number came up for me to tell a childhood story naked. I don't remember the specifics of the story, but I do know that I took off my clothes without compunction. By then, I wasn't too bothered by nudity and actually kind of enjoyed it. After years of negotiating undress, I'd come to feel grounded and strong in my body on stage with clothes on or off. Performance art had emphasized being in my body as opposed to appearing in it: what I was doing rather than how I looked. At the same time, I had a sense that I looked pretty fucking good. My time in Mexico walking, wandering, dancing, and having good sex had changed my body in positive ways.

As a black feminist, I try hard not to get caught up in bullshit beauty standards (and often fail); still changing my body in Mexico was never a conscious goal. However, I did want to improve my relationship to my body off the stage and being in Mexico allowed me the opportunity to do so. I had pleasure in my body in Mexico and felt better in my body, which helped me look better to myself. My body looked good naked in *Tie Air*. Or at least I thought so. (*Who can really say what our bodies mean to anyone else? Or actually what they look like?*)

This moment of nudity in *Tie Air* marked and shifted something for me as a black feminist performance artist in Minnesota. For so long, I'd struggled to have a body there, to feel like something more than a desexed brain, or a racialized unsuccessful sex object. Performance art had helped a lot, but lasting embodiment was hard to land. In Minnesota, I often felt disregarded and disassociated. I felt the opposite of those things in *Tie Air*. More than feeling vulnerable in my nudity or even empowered (a word often used in feminist debates around sexuality and objectification), I felt *present*, less conspicuous and more integrated, even if still somewhat unintelligible. Later my colleague Cecilia said that *Tie Air* felt different from any other performance of mine and it felt that way to me too. A concentration of presence and absence. "We hadn't seen you in forever," Cecilia said, "then you came to town, got naked, and left." It was true. I didn't know if my shifted presence would hold or how my transformation could possibly play out. How would this new me fare in Minnesota? I didn't wait to find out.

A few days after *Tie Air*, I returned to Mexico.

143

March 20, 2009
Subject: tocada

Marco!
How fantastic to hear from you . . . I can't believe March
is already coming to an end and April is around the corner.
My mother just sent me my parents' itinerary for a nice
Mexico visit. They are coming Friday April 10 and leaving
the following Saturday. I can't wait! My father is fluent in
Spanish but says it's been years since he's been in a solely
Spanish speaking country (he's a French and Spanish high
school teacher) so I can't wait to see him in action--and my
mother is going to throw down at the Mercado Medellin right
next to my house. She loves fruit and flowers and seafood
and connecting with sellers so I imagine we'll have a lot of
fun!

So many things to report! First off, my new jirafa oaxaqueña
is staring down at my fingers as I type this. I was walking
back from the gym when I saw a lady braiding colored straw
into fanciful animals. She didn't try to sell me anything,
she was just sitting there doing her thing and I actually
walked past when I swear to you--my little jirafa screamed
out--Oye! Quiero ir contigo morena!" And do you know, I
turned around and plopped down twenty pesos on the spot.
Sometimes it's like that.

Next, I have no running water in my house. Although everyone
else in my building does. It's a pesky problem that pops up
whenever I need to take a hot shower (often accompanied by
a lack of gas or the pilot light not lighting). Una doña
in the building who sits outside, sells dulces, and sees
everyone's business, told me it was probably a problem with
my cisterna--but it's frustrating because I just got back
to Mexico earlier this week and I want to feel grounded,
settled (and of course clean!)

Part of that was accomplished when I finally was able to
make the garbage man's bell. I couldn't get the trash out
before I left--and so it was waiting for me out on the
patio. I hate the trash! But I like a  clean house even
more--so I did it--and even got a wolf whistle on the way to
the corner seeing as I'm wearing a zebra print sundress and

my hair is crazy (due to lack of said water to style it--see above.)

I just got back from doing two very intense things in the Twin Cities. First, I got to introduce Rita Dove at a huge reading at my College. You can look on Facebook to see pictures of me with la Paloma. Have you ever met her? She is the coolest, most gracious, kindest, down to earth poet I've ever met. And she meant so much to me in my journey to poetry, it was really a dream come true. I had her inscribe a book to my Mom and my mother was so excited, she took it to the hairdresser and sorority meeting and everywhere. So all of that was cool.

The other thing was that I showed the new performance art derived from and inspired by my time here in Mexico and especially my wild experiences with La Congelada in the taller and my fear and anxiety about leaving the vital, vibrant sexy Mexico Gabrielle behind to return to the drab, invisible Gabrielle. There was dancing with candy in our shoes. Me eating 5 minutes of ice in real time. Rolling around in ice to Purple Rain. Showing very short videos of my eyeballs, my hands "tying air," my tongue French kissing a caddish Mexican lothario and more. Good times! Or also known as complete and total emotional trainwreck after which I'm still recovering.;-)

I plan to take the show to Puerto Rico and maybe if I can squeeze somewhere in New York. I just need a confederate to play the Congelada role. I'll let you know if it comes to your town. (Or maybe you and Daff can bring me.)

What else? Daniel H and I are planning to go to a poetry reading that I was invited to by a guy I met on the pesero on the way to make the said Mexican French kiss video. I hope Dani ends up coming because I haven't seen him in a while.

I was gone for two weeks in the US (did I mention the blizzard in Atlanta! the lost computer! the frozen bank account! Okay, I just did--so we can move on). I was struck by how freaked out everyone was about the economy. I'm a pretty good budgeter and saver (although I have absolutely no problem heeding the call of a jirafa from Oaxaca-- see above--or getting yummy tacos or blue nail polish or

145

whatever but even with all this, I'm pretty good with money)
and yet I felt like I wanted to swear off all worldly
possessions, melt down my gold hoops into bars, grab all
my cash and store it under my bed. People in (that part of
North) America are freaked out! So that was interesting.

Which brings us to the Fulbright. My fingers are still
definitely crossed for you. . . . My jirafa is sending you
good energy and so am I. (He is also a rattle--which means
he's on the same onda as your músicos veracruzanos. . .)

So keep me posted on all that happens. And please send my
best to Daffodil. She is so lovely in pictures! I can't
wait to meet her. I am off tomorrow to Puerto Morelos for
a weeklong yoga retreat and then am back to prepare for at
least one performance (hopefully two) and three workshops.
Then I am going to REST!!!!

Abrazos,
Gabrielle

Gracias al Sr. de la Salud por la revelación de mi
segundo chacra durante el retiro de yoga en Puerto
Morelos, que mucho me ayudo para mi recupera-
ción, despues del duro trabajo que tube que realizar
para preparar mi performance "TIE AIR" EN "MINEAPOLIS" y
tambien para prepararme para mis proximas aventuras
amorosas en Mexico. 21 DE MARZO DE 2009
                                   PUERTO MORELOS MEXICO.

# LENGUA

My Spanish wasn't terrible when I came to Mexico, but it was honestly pretty weird.

After years of French, mi "accento" était très bizarre and I'd jumble up words from different languages. Mind you, this didn't stop me from running around and making friends. In fact, my first friends in Mexico were at language schools. During my sabbatical in 2007, I studied Spanish with other gringos and Eastern and Western Europeans, first in Playa del Carmen and then in Mexico City. We all got to hang out together with Mexican teachers at evening mixers over snacks and beer. Little did I know that those teachers would be kind enough to confirm my language competency for my Fulbright application. My Spanish had to be good enough to complete my project, or at least that's what the Fulbright needed to believe.

In reality, my strange speech acts at the beginning of my Fulbright year could charm or puzzle native listeners. I would say *embrazo* instead of *abrazo*, pronounce *en* like *ahn*, mess up a subjunctive tense, or freeze in the face of an unknown word. People would offer corrections or explanations and, more often than not, my language foibles would turn into a comedy gag. (Yet again, I played the fool). Sometimes though, my words, or attempts at words, led to complete confusion. It still stings remembering a curator's remark that my language was *ininteligible*. Whatever I was trying to say about my art dissolved and shame flushed throughout my body.

Living in a different language can feel like constantly taking a test. You're always on the verge of being wrong, hyperaware of everything you don't know. Nevertheless, without you always thinking about it, a different language seeps into your skin. An ñ shapes your mouth; a double R moves your feet. This can become the rhythm of your life.

My friend Allison, an artist and theorist of multilingual education, talks about the difference between language accuracy and fluency. Speaking perfectly isn't the same as speaking well, which is really speaking without hesitation, speaking all the time.

I made mistakes in Spanish just as I did in Mexico.

I got lost in language sometimes and couldn't find my way. Or others couldn't find me. Truth be told, I also still spoke a fair amount of English with other Fulbrighters and expatriate friends. However, I spoke Spanish all the time and, over time, my Spanish got better, clearer, more automatic, more organic. I whispered sweet nothings in Spanish to lovers in bed, had lover's quarrels and made plans, read books and bartered badly, gave lectures and performed with musicians, daydreamed and listened to the radio. I spoke with frequency, on a different frequency. So my relationship to Spanish, and my Spanish itself, grew more embodied, natural, and alive.

Although I now live in Los Angeles where Spanish speakers abound, I rarely speak Spanish anymore. My language came from the surround, the vibrations of the place, the rhythms of my life there. I will never be a native speaker, but, for a little while, Spanish moved inside my tongue.

# ASIDE (SEX FEVER DF)

*(I arrived in la Cuidad de México, Distrito Federal on a one way ticket, knowing absolutely nobody. It didn't take long for me to fall in love . . . )*

It usually isn't hard for me
to meet new people in a new place
I arrive and explore, turn up at a show
or just standing in line or walking down the street
I can lock eyes and wink or start chatting
and one thing leads to another

I met L. on the way to Sanborn's
to get some chicken tortilla soup
He asked me if I had the time
(sometime later, when we were naked
I spied the watch on his wrist)
His body was wiry and firm
His penis, long and effective
Like clockwork, he showed up for sex

I met F. when I walked into a little taqueria
He was reading poems and eating a torta
He looked up and smiled
We started to chat in Spanish
and turned to English
He translated me
We never had sex
but it still felt hot

I did have sex
with D. whom I met
at a performance art show
protesting U.S. genetic
modification of corn
in vivid violet gestures

and with C. whom I dated
and with whom I fussed
and fought and swooned
over that corny song
mi unicornio azul
when he crooned it to me
one sweet, boozy night

and with E. whom I loved
kissing the spider tattoos
on his neck and the snakes
below his belly button
made stars twinkle under my skin
and he seemed to really see me

and lover, I should have stayed over
for sunday comida with his family
but had to get home
so I sent him poems instead

And you have to understand:
I am not usually flirty or brassy
the naïve star of a rom com
or raunchy sex romp

I am either a well put together
bougie boho black boss
or a complete disaster nerd
with unpainted nails, unruly hair
and 16 books in my bag

But I was so in love
with the world
then and there
desired and desiring
curious and open
happy to be in heat
living dreams
pulsing with body

# DESIRE PATHS

*(Barack Obama was not the only man
who captured my attention in Mexico. . . . )*

The trajectory of my sexuality has taken many twists and turns, experienced serious expansion and retraction. While lately, I've been rocking a robust art nun life, hot tea in the morning and fuzzy socks in bed at night, I have felt and do feel attraction for many different people (in different genders, hues, sizes, shapes, languages, and nationalities). My time in Mexico reminds me of the ardor of desire. How things could be different for me, how in fact I have been different. In Mexico, I was BOYCRAZY! Still a hardcore feminist (sisterhood is powerful), I had more male friends than ever before in my life. Moreover, for once, boys acted crazy about me. Without much effort, it felt like I was beating them off with a stick (or my hand or my . . . you get the point). I was having hot juicy sex with wondrous, specific individuals with opinions and quirks and hard, beautiful bodies who acted like they weren't doing me a favor. Like maybe I was doing them one. And please forgive me for crowing about this because, believe me, in the United States of America that was not usually my deal. (¡Dorothy, ya no estás en Kansas! O en mi caso, Minnesota . . .)

Don't get me wrong. I never achieved true sluttiness. In my twenties, my goal to become *The Ethical Slut* was foiled because 1) not enough people wanted to sleep with me 2) my feelings got hurt and 3) I don't like to wait around. The algorithm of the U.S. desire index placed me—black, plump, female, dreamy, mouthy, and brainy—in the friend zone or as the third wheel, the sassy sidekick, the secret side chick, or the beard. None of that was good enough. I wanted my own lovers, but I didn't want to be treated like shit. That was the rub. So I stepped back from flesh: read, wrote, and sublimated my desire. I made intricate performance art and traveled around the world.

A funny thing happened outside the U.S.

My body was allowed to become something else.

Of course cultural differences were at play,

different tastes and proclivities.

U.S. standards of beauty, femininity, masculinity, gender identity, racial appeal, and desirability itself, are profoundly oppressive: this cannot be overstated. Leaving the US doesn't solve racism, misogyny, homophobia, transphobia, fatphobia, cruelty, stupidity, small-mindedness, misguided YouTube tutorials, or bad manners; and it certainly doesn't prevent exploitation or fetish. But it did allow for the creation of different desire paths: you know the routes we make when we move where we want and not where we're supposed to go. (*Too often, for me as a black woman, my geography has arrived already circumscribed . . .*)

So many voices around me had said: slim yourself down, doll yourself up, play a little dumb and rose petals will fall from the sky. With some changes, even you could be desired.

As it turned out, I didn't change a thing about myself.

I just needed to be somewhere else.

When I lived in Mexico, I was out of my usual box. Maybe I landed in a foreigner box, a dumb gringo box, an exoticized black female box, or a box I never even knew. (Who can really say what our bodies mean to anyone else?) But just the possibility of being seen in a new way, being seen at all and not disregarded, opened a new space of desire for me. My body was appreciated as it arrived. The radio dial turned and I got picked up with a different frequency. My body hummed.

# DEVIL DANCE

« Negro, emporte-moi dans tes ténèbres . . . Oh le diable, l'enfer, le nègre ! »
—Sami Tchak, *Filles de Mexico*

\*

One day, I stumbled onto a festival of Afro-Mexican culture in Parque Mexico.

Black and white images of Afro-Mexicans from the Costa Chica and Veracruz hung larger than life over the bandshell. In one photo, a naked boy sits on his mother's shoulders. In another, two brown niños laugh and smile. My favorite image shows two black women, both with unmistakable Negro hair. One wears a gold chain around her neck. The other sports a metal pendant on a cord. Unlike the other images, the women are not questioning or confronting the camera. They face each other, standing in front of a body of water. They could be in Haiti or Senegal or New Orleans. This still moves me deeply.

This was the first public display I'd seen in Mexico of people who looked like me. Even now, I can't recall any other examples (except maybe the movie poster for *Traitor* with Don Cheadle). Freedom from the white gaze had been a balm. Still, I definitely missed seeing blackness.

In Mexico, my own blackness was seen all the time.
Spotted, glimpsed, noticed, spied,
witnessed, captured, and remarked.
That just comes with the territory.

Part of my job as a black feminist performance artist is to navigate presence. I was used to dealing with invisibility and hypervisibility (after all, I'd lived for years as a black woman in Minnesota . . . .) However, in Mexico, my blackness was spectacular. *"¿De dónde eres?"* (Where are you from?) people asked me everywhere I went. Sometimes people stared. Strangers would take my picture without asking. Not because I was a celebrity: just because I was black. When my uncle came to visit, a woman studying ethnography stopped us at lunch and asked to take a picture with us for a school report. (We agreed in exchange for us taking her picture too.) At cantinas, men, often tipsy, always asked me to dance. Children sometimes balked at the sight of me. That made me feel like the devil.

*

While living in Mexico City, I was obsessed with this book called *Filles de Mexico*. Written by Sami Tchak from Togo, it came out in 2008, the same year as my Fulbright fellowship. As far as I know, it is the only West African novel in French about hanging out in Mexico City. (If you know of others, please tell me because I want to read those books.) Living in a Spanish-speaking country and speaking a lot of English with expatriate pals, I didn't want to lose my French, so I read it slowly, savoring the story. Describing a Togolese man's experience of blackness in Mexico City, *Filles de Mexico* aligned perfectly with so many things whirling in my head. The title translates as Mexican Girls (or Mexican Daughters) or even Girls in Mexico and, it features a lot of cross-cultural sexual escapades.

In the novel, girls run up to the West African narrator and want to touch his black skin, get him drunk, and have their way. In one memorable episode, he goes into a bar with friends and says:

« Notre arrivé attira l'attention de tout le monde. Pepe était un habitué des lieux, c'était surtout moi qui devenais un élément insolite dans ce décor. Negro, ah Negro ! Le bar s'emplit des Negro, Negro. »

"Our arrival caught everyone's attention. Pepe was a regular, so I was the one out of place. Negro, ah Negro! The bar swells with Negro, Negro."

As heightened as this description may seem, that "Negro, Negro" struck a chord with me. At different times in my life, I had seen racial presence become a spectator sport and suck up all the space in the room. I had come to Mexico to explore my own racial meaning in a different place, but this novel showed how it could take a monstrous turn. When a pregnant woman snubs the narrator in the bar, he decides to mouth off. First, he brings up "el tercer raíz," Mexico's official recognition of African culture as "the third root" of Mexican culture (after European and indigenous cultures). Then the narrator suggests that Adela, the pregnant woman, will be the first Mexican girl to have the third root implanted inside her. (« Eh ben, Adela, tu seras la première Mexicaine à la planter en toi. »)

The idea that the African narrator is the father of Adela's unborn baby makes the bar crowd roar with laughter. After another guy in the bar makes up a dirty song about pregnant Adela getting fucked and starving Africans being ravaged by viruses (yeah, really funny), Adela lashes out and basically says to the singer, "Fuck you! I'd rather be with the Negro than you." Then in a flash, Adela slips from disgust to desire:

« Negro, emporte-moi dans tes ténèbres, s'il te plaît, emporte-moi en enfer, je veux ta queue, je veux la queue du diable ! Oh le diable, l'enfer, le nègre ! »

"Negro, sweep me into your darkness, please, take me to hell, I want your cock, I want the cock of the devil. Oh the devil, hell, the black man."

Here, the African narrator, "Negro," changes from a cock (the third root) into "the devil, hell, the black man."

To get some peace, he runs off to the loo, only to have an obese Mexican woman follow him and demand to have sex with him right there. *I want to have sex with the devil*, she says. He gives up, gives in, and gets into it. He gets it up and gets it in. The black devil fucks the fat Mexicana in a dirty bathroom stall. Is this an inspiring example of cultural exchange? an affirmation of cultural pride? Tchak's writing is filthy, funny and wry, maybe even a little sad.

With its caricatures and vulgarity, *Filles de Mexico* sometimes made me squirm but it made me think hard about race and desire, how blackness circulated in Mexico. What is the impact of cultural claims? Where do objectification, stereotype, and pleasure meet? On a personal note, how do I negotiate fetish? What exactly do others see when they see me? For liberation and desire: there might be the devil to pay.

*

"The devil dance is the most widely publicized dance of the Afro-Mexican Costa Chica. The hairy, masked character that dominates the dance fascinates tourists. Behind the mask of the Devil, Afro-Mexicans are able to restructure—albeit briefly—the social hierarchies that circumscribe their daily lives."

—Anita González, Afro-Mexico, *Dancing Between Myth and Reality*

In Parque Mexico, the masked dancers took the stage in their colorful costumes. They wore traditional masks with long devil's hair moustaches. Their horns were bright and sparkly as were their windbreakers, deliberately tattered, each dancer clad in a different color, royal blue, fuchsia, orange, and red. The devil in red was the one who saw me in the audience. The music was playing and they were starting their dance. *Bailamos con nosotros.* I looked both ways. As far as I could tell, I was the only black person in the audience. They called me to the stage out of the blue, me in long sleeves and heavy blue jeans. It wasn't a demand, ("Negro, Negro") but a public recognition. I didn't know this devil dance, had never seen it before, had read about it in books, had admired it from afar. I wasn't Afro-Mexican, couldn't really be sure what it would mean. Everyone was watching. Black is beautiful. I did the best I could.

# FROM MY NOTEBOOKS

performagia

> international festival
> of performance art 2009
>               May 5-10
>       TLAXCALA, MEXICO
> sponsored by Museo Universitario del CHOPO...

 8 abril 09
A couple months ago I got a call from the fabulous Pancho López –
SHHH!
I'm going to tell
you a secret -
we are inviting
you to perform at this
year's Performagia...
(*on the side of the page*)  HOORAY I said.

Now in less than a month, I will be showing work in Tlaxcala – opening the festival and offering 3 workshops on performance –
        May God give me STRENGTH!
And yet I feel like I've come to a reckoning –
        I don't want to just redo BRUSH or something else... I want to offer some-
thing new – but something that would be on the trajectory I've been building
over the course of the year – what will then culminate in In and Out of Place...
        this performance is less diva, less hip hop, less wry, less spectacular than
the next one –
        this is to be the RACE performance
        something about the silly – the loopy – the mysterious
        what Madhu told me she read about Kate Bush:
         loopy, precious, and big hearted

*

Possible Titles for this show

| | | |
|---|---|---|
| tonal shift | cannibalism | negrita |
| contrast | dessert | lullaby |
| threshold | -costa chica- | blackface |
| smear - | dream          disjuncture | espejo |
| creation myth | the most surprising thing | the secret life of la negríta? |
| origin story | that could happen – or we could discover | |

THINGS I KNOW SO FAR
the negrita doll is the muse
        this is something about her secret
history and possibility
            Faith Ringgold and what she did with Aunt Jemima and that quilt –
more LOOPY and LESS EARNEST
        Reclamation
but also turning inside out
move away from a flat multicultural piece – something about what they see
make them see something in a new way
                        possibility
THRESHOLD ---------> people arrive and I offer hugs in this guise
        and I'm hugging everyone and passing out <u>Negritos</u> –
something is playing in the background --------> blurb from Bamboozled –
blackface? ---or the video of me being made up like this – and it's on slow motion
so I'm unseen at first – but what they see is the rubbing into the face – close up <---

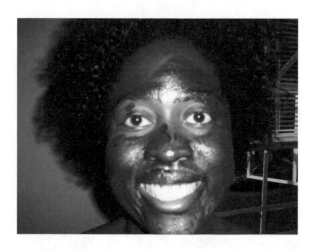

# I'm in the concept – just have to keep working it

what are the key actions and images?
How to understand/uncover/create the creation myth of this woman
la negrita

<u>OBAMA BUTTON</u>

eating the <u>negrito</u>     (*written vertically on the side*) or is it falling black feathers?
(*on the diagonal*) that part of Berlitz that no one understood
encuentro                          reverse/black snow
cannibalism                        ego tripping
creation myth
inside out                                   black magic ------------> turn into something else
l'origine du monde
meditations on slavery                       transformation
layering                                     concept  image  action

la negrita sneaks off for a date -
she hugs you or sings a lullaby for you to go to sleep
and while you're sleeping, she sneaks off to her lover -
she prepares for this date
is he there?
Does he stand her up?
Is it a tragic story?                          (Karen Finley -"we keep our
Does she overeat to feel better?                        victims ready")

162

And Molly saying – next time tell a story
BEDTIME STORY

----- maybe you get milk and a little piece of a cookie
maybe it's about perversion/recursion – explosion of the material
but some other
historical shit that -----          snacks
goes along with this              treats
                                  warmth


* * *


does it start with a mask and then I become it for real?
          Childhood – caring for someone else's jump rope?
Al Jolson ---->          Oh mammy, I'll sing about you
All the pretty little horses
          Kathleen Battle
Johnny Weissmuller Tarzan call       cheetah's jungle dance
– live African drummer ---------> eating the Negrito
(*on the side of the page*) García Lorca play --------------> napkins over the spoons
                                  read the poem ---->
It's amazing how in a short time, you can make progress
- stop freaking out and do your work! –


April 13, 2009
          I've been fighting lethargy, fear, paralysis, anxiety to sit down and do
this work. Part of me believes it will all work out – another part thinks it will
be something good but not really good – another part is channeling the Great
Brain – believes while I sleep or sweep the floor or watch Friday Night Lights
(Atmospherics), that key elements are churning their way into place.
          it all will happen . . . I just have to remember:


# I WAS BORN
## to do this . . .
# B R A V E  J O Y !


163

April 14, 2009

     I feel GOOD this morning – really good! And now I know the answer
----> get up EARLY shower dress and march into the <u>day</u>. I got the
PERFORMAGIA schedule today and I see the whole gang doing stuff in the
DF and I'm queen of Tlaxcala – It's okay to be far away since I'm going to have
my <u>triumph</u> at Ex Teresa (¡Ojala!) later that month – and all the hip defeños will
come rock it –

     I feel capable this morning and determined. By Sunday – the "script" of
this piece will be done – the sequence – the elements and the form turned in – I
can deepen the sections or switch things later – but I don't need to overthink this
– both because it won't make the piece better (and will likely make it worse) and
because I have another piece a few weeks later.

The name of the piece is

MUÑO ------> (I summon)

from the verb muñir

good title because it brings in the moon – when the moon comes out –

the negrita transforms/becomes someone [else/more herself]

Moon yo Muñeca – mist ---> shackle

doll   negrita doll

slips away

has a moment to herself

prepares for her evening out

her cosmic lover to arrive ------- clandestine meeting

awaits bliss ------ a shower of STARS?

right – thinking about the pieces – kind of proceeding – talking a lot about them
but not getting much done. What does it mean to "get something done" – I'm
not sure. I'm interested in Bartolomé's taller but wonder if it's a bad idea. It's
either <u>exactly</u> what I need or exactly <u>not</u>.

I wish I had the footage of my grandmother and Haiti from RSVP – it feels to
me like that's a part of Muño – but I don't think I have it, maybe if I think of my
grandmother – the piece will fall into place. I also keep thinking of the solo in
<u>Laura's Summer Ballet</u> when the painting comes to life.

It's raining outside and everyone is nuts about the swine flu. C. was sick at
the end of last week and still doesn't feel 100% - so I called him to make sure
he's okay – It seemed like a fluke thing but now there's talk of a real epidemic
– there's a real <u>panic</u> – I bought my "cubrabocas" and hand sanitizer and feel a
little sheepish but also concerned.

Mon, Apr 27, 2009 at 5:47 PM
Google Chat

5:16 PM me: Hey Marcoooooo!
 I'm speaking to you from beneath a blue face mask.
5:30 PM Marco: Gabbsssss... I've been on the phone. How was
your facial? How are you? What's the deal with this flu
thing?
5:31 PM me: Ha! I wish my blue face mask were a facial as
opposed to a surgical half mask to combat the swine flu.
   The city has gone crazy.
   And the whole country too.
   ALL SCHOOLS IN MEXICO COUNTRY ARE CLOSED FOR 10 DAYS!
   Not just Mexico city!
5:32 PM Marco: What are you going to do? Stay?
 me: Yeah. . . this is my home.
   I'm still preparing two performances and a workshop.
   And I don't have anywhere else to go.
5:33 PM Besides, the chance of me getting swine flu
seems really really small. Although to be honest, I don't
feel that well today--probably a result of paranoia and
pollution.
 Marco: Daffodil showing me Daniel's npr thing now.
 me: Yes Daniel's been documenting it all really well.
   How are the two of you?
5:34 PM You and Daffodil?
5:35 PM Marco: We're cool. Wondering if we could get pet
chihuahua flu over here, having been exposed to a fat little
dog.
me: :-)
Have you guys set a date on the wedding?
5:37 PM Oops... Around new year's eve.
It's a great time to get folks to Taxco. . .
5:42 PM me: sooo exciting! lemme know if you come into town.
I have an extra bedroom if you two need a place to stay.
 Marco: awwwww. thanks.
 me: Am exhausted from my day in the epicenter of the
epidemic.
      Gotta run
5:49 PM but it's good to chat with you--2009-2010 FULBRIGHT
FELLOW!
 Marco: ah! take good care of yourself.
5:50 PM me: chau (wawa) ;-)

# SWINE FLU

We wore masks over our mouths and stayed inside. Almost everything was shut down. Some abarrotes were open and maybe big grocery stores. I wasn't sure. I didn't really go anywhere. Some of my U.S. friends went back home, but I had just been there and didn't have the money. I didn't want to travel anyway. My big shows were coming up and my creativity was starting to surge. Performance art wouldn't make itself, right? My Spanish had gotten better, so I was reading the newspaper, listening on the radio to some news. Still, I didn't really understand. It didn't make sense. I was living in one of the biggest, most badass cities in the world.

Where were the pigs?

What was the swine flu?

It made me think of "Bird Flu," that banging song by M.I.A that I would listen to LOUD, driving to teach at St. Kate's. Outside it was Minnesota, but inside my car it was "Bamboo Banga," "Bird Flu, "World Town," and "Paper Planes." I loved that album so much. A global smash! I'd play it in my apartment on Coahuila that year. Global hip hop mingling with the sounds of organ grinders outside my window. Their Harmonipans churned out of tune while tamale vendors called out their flavors, and shoppers chatted and hummed their way over to the Mercado Medellín next door. Resounding daily life.

Then, just like that, the streets were silent. The only time I lived in Mexico with no surround sound. No cars on the road. No bustling people. No one I knew had gotten sick, but people were dying. It was in the air. Over the airwaves. No one I knew was using the word *pandemic*. But that had been declared. International noise. I understood something crucial about US media when NPR turned to a fellow Fulbrighter for the local story. *Can you report what's going on there in Mexico City?* She spoke with authority. But what did she know? She was an artist like me. Why were they asking her? Was just being American enough? Or the fact that she could speak perfect, unaccented English?

This was a foreign experience.
Like SARS or MERS,
it was something those other people got.
My family in the U.S. asked me:
*What is going on there? How are you feeling?*
*We heard on the news that there's a disease.*
It was that far away.

*

(Years later, another epidemic would come,
another something those other people got
and this time it hits home and shuts us down
and locks us in and steals our elders
and addles our youth and targets our breath
and masks our faces and disappears our legs
and breaks our hearts and robs us of rituals
and seals us off and makes us remote
and grows our hair long and flabs our bellies
and shuts down our economy and loses our jobs
and cancels our plays and depresses our spirits
and befuddles and overwhelms and terrifies
and divides and closes us in everywhere closer
but the swine flu barely registered
back then to the folks back home
and while it certainly impacted my life
when conjuring memories
of my magical Mexico year
it barely surfaces at all.)

April 28, 2009 And so this is it ----> being a performance artist for real.  Getting up – cleaning up/trashing the house – answering correspondence – sending off proposals – writing in my journal – doing yoga – emptying the space – walking into the empty space and trying to square the imagination with actions – I feel weirdly more grounded conceptually in the other piece – although the logistics there are nightmarish – But this piece for which I have all of the elements – feels absolutely flat – boring – predictable – unalive – the good news is that I have the time – the vision to make it work – and today is the day when I will do it!

Monday May 4, 2009  8:05 PM
       Today has been a momentous day for Muño – I almost love it now (and
think that once I get more grounded and rehearsed, I will love it – I almost know
it – I showed it to both Laura M and in the next stage Daniel H. - and I feel more
clear about the parts and the work that needs to be done.


What Laura M did
-----> watched me fumble                     Muño expense sheet
-----> stayed calm and kind                      1100 pesos costume
-----> helped me edit and               485 pesos rum and coffee
organize the pre-songs                        100 pesos silver container
–help me crystallize my
ritual / decision not to                          Key problem areas:
use cups/have a toast                           –script with slides
but create a ritual                                  –antropofagia ------>
–helped me edit and reorder                       negrito
–helped me sequence the show slides


What Daniel did
 ----> saw the whole thing and liked it
-----> emphasized the power of the costume
-----> also questioned the negrito
-----> Be slower and more deliberate with the costume
-----> add the slides underneath the Negro de la Costa/antropofagia
section
-----> reconsider the hyperbole of the negrito

  Do you look at the audience?
  Do you take awareness of them?
  Do you take care of them?
  Do you play to them?

Maybe that's part of it too ---->
PLAYING VS PLAYING TO OR PLAYING FOR
the play is the thing       Press Play – activate

TONAL SHIFTS
and this is a piece where I really need to trust myself:
"Hacer lo que viene de adentro sin miedo y <u>sin contemplarlo demasiado</u>"
        - Amat Escalante
This is so key – to have some nerves but also to arrive prepared, ready, and
        excited -
I'll rehearse the piece again or mark it – walk through – 2x3 times closer to the
        date ------>
        But I want to keep it FRESH and what it was

KEEP PUSHING
EDIT
GET MANY OPINIONS
DON'T GIVE UP
GET GROUNDED
LESS IS MORE
as in the *taller* ----> let them enjoy me

\* \* \*

7:42 PM 6 mayo 2009
# IF IT WAS MY DREAM TO LIVE/BE AS AN ARTIST, I AM LIVING BEING MY DREAM

* * *

So much to write about.  All of this is a part of it.
2009 a year of wonders!
Laura Edith is getting married!
Yesterday Eric Leigh called –
His BOOK WAS  ACCEPTED FOR PUBLICATION! YAHOOOO!
                    We are all entering the heart of life.

I don't have my books yet.  I don't have my great love.  But I also don't feel left
behind.  I have this – the practice and opportunity of fostering visions – aiming to
integrate movement, image, language, event. I get to do this –  increasingly – on a
world stage. This Muño performance, the passion – focus of my life right now

  "The harder you work, the more talented you become" - Faith Ringgold

* * *

<--oh no! the biggest shock – I won't be going to Tlaxcala! Ahhh!
the whole PERFORMAGIA festival in Tlaxcala se suspendió - is up
in the air  – due to the swine flu, it's possibly cancelled– probably
postponed until next week –

* * *

Now – on to Francis Taylor
Who is beautiful and pierced and black
I could see the band of his underpants the first time we met.
He blushed. In the DR he works with people with AIDS
he works on issues of discrimination
against people with AIDS.
so kind and cool
and who I hope will be my friend over time...
Francis is here in DF braving the swine flu
to perform in Performagia
Sitting in a chair at the bottom of a stone stairwell,
he read a long letter in a calm, soothing voice.
He read it slowly – with emotion but not excess animation.
Due to an echo in el Eco, strange distortion in the video, etc.
we could not understand a word.
He was there and also not there

171

# ENTENDER

Performance as a man reading a letter
     as a black man reading a letter
         a moreno reading a letter
         in an ornate chair
     a Dominican reading a letter where the word Mexico can be heard
     a brown skinned man reading a letter
         we don't understand
     a foreigner reading a letter
     that our machinery can't decipher
     a video of an artist reading an unintelligible letter
     an unintelligible video
     an unintelligible artist
     an unintelligible reading
     an unintelligible letter
         we can't
              nadie lo entiende
                 no entendimos nada
     he was clear in the space
     but we can't understand
     do we need to?

     on the video, he stops reading
         he opens up his shirt
         and I see his chest
         exactly how I imagined it
         when he pulled himself up
         on the trapeze and did a flip
         turned his legs up over his head
         at the centro cultural roma

     over his heart a passel of small pins
         were stuck into his skin.  candy
         colored pin tops. blue. yellow. pink.
         he pulls them out slowly and sticks
         them into a small red pin cushion.
         we see the small ragged holes

of flesh where pins used to be
I don't understand

what do these pins in his heart
        their revelation and removal
        – in slow time –
        have to do with that letter?
        I don't understand
        but imagine dots of blood

He moves toward the audience
        – sees a young woman
        offers her the red pin cushion
        and she pulls out a pin
        and passes the velvet along
        he sheds the object/material
        is he now more intelligible?
        he turns and walks away

# Desde un costado de la caja
## Una reflexión en torno a dos obras de Gabrielle Civil
## por Pancho López

1

Con su obra performática Gabrielle Civil ha hecho una reflexión sobre sí misma. Su obra es un espejo. Resultado de una profunda observación se va trazando un autorrecorrido. Se sabe negra, se sabe fuerte, se sabe bella. Las autorreferencias son el menú que se ofrece sobre la mesa.

*Muño / Fantasía de la negrita* es resultado de esta revisión. En esta obra se apropia de íconos populares y los habita, transformándose en un personaje conocido por todos, chicos y grandes ¿es la negrita de los Hot Cakes? ¿Es la muñequita de trapo con su ropa roja de bolitas? El modo en que ella observa es performático, su actitud coleccionista a partir de una mirada selectiva. Caza imágenes y las recorta haciendo con ello un gran collage, un rompecabezas con el que intenta dar forma a su identidad.

Si bien la negritud en la Ciudad de México está negada, es casi invisible de no ser por algún par de turistas que visitan o pequeñas comunidades caribeñas aisladas aposentadas en zonas de la Santa María, por las calles del Distrito Federal es excepcional ver a gente de color. Sin embargo, la ciudad es profundamente racista, clasista y sectaria; como en muchos lugares del mundo el código postal influye para los asuntos del día a día. Aunque cabe señalar que la raíz negra en México se remite a la costa chica de Guerrero, y a algunas zonas también aisladas de Oaxaca y Veracruz.

Justo en este marco es dónde se inserta la presencia de Civil, justo en las comisuras que rozan lo exótico, lo inusual, e incluso la caricatura. Ver por la calle a una mujer negra, femenina, con grandes ojos, cabellos crespos y silueta detallada es la fantasía de muchos varones, y es que en este país tan machista el deseo es alimentado por revistas que intensifican la imaginación de una clase no muy privilegiada. Pero ella se burla, se inserta en la calle integrando experiencias y situaciones, mas bien generándolas.

Esa negrita habita un cuerpo que no es suyo. Es quizás el de su abuela, quien bebía ron. En Muño el ron funciona como un bálsamo catalizador, como un medio para traer en el tiempo la esencia de la abuela de Civil. Limpiándose las manos con ron, uno a uno van entrando los espectadores, va paulatinamente realizándose el ritual, entre granos de café y música, entre recuerdos e imágenes, se va develando esa identidad con raíces haitianas. Con estas acciones, la presencia se (re) semantiza y obtiene un valor distinto. Se habla de la necesidad de pertenencia, de identidad, de la importancia de tener un origen y un sentido de la vida.

El cuerpo será siempre un espacio de revisión, un escenario, una cancha. Ahí se han de presentar cientos de situaciones–tanto públicas como privadas–dónde se cuestionen, se desdoblen y se develen problemáticas y pensamientos profundos.

# From a Side of the Box
## An essay on two works by Gabrielle Civil
## by Pancho López
## translated by Lucía Abolafia Cobo

1

With her performance work, Gabrielle Civil has done a self-analysis. Her work is a mirror. An inner journey mapped from deep observation. She knows herself as black, she knows herself as strong, she knows herself as beautiful. Self-references are the menu offerings on the table.

*Muño / Fantasía de la Negrita* is the result of this study. In this work, Civil takes over popular icons and inhabits them by becoming a character known to everyone, young and old. Is she the black lady on the pancake box? Is she the rag doll in a red polka dot dress? Her mode of observation is performance. Her collector's attitude arises from a selective gaze. She hunts for images and cuts them up to create a large collage, a puzzle she uses to shape her identity.

Because negritude in Mexico City is denied—it is almost invisible except for a couple of visiting tourists or in some small Caribbean communities in the Santa María neighborhood—it is exceptional to see black people in the streets of Mexico City. Moreover, the city is deeply racist, classist and sectarian; just as in many parts of the world, the zip code influences daily affairs. Although, it must be noted that black roots in Mexico are found in the Costa Chica of Guerrero, as well as some isolated parts of Oaxaca and Veracruz.

Precisely in this context, Civil's presence becomes embedded, right on the border that brushes against the exotic, the unusual and even the cartoonish. To see a black, feminine woman with big eyes and curly hair and a well-detailed silhouette walking on the streets is the fantasy of many men. Magazines feed off that desire in a chauvinist country where the imagination of a not-so-privileged class is intensified. Nonetheless, she mocks it and embeds herself on the streets by integrating experiences and situations, or better yet by creating them.

That *Negrita* inhabits a body that doesn't belong to her. It is perhaps that of her grandmother, who used to drink rum. In *Muño*, rum is used as a catalyst balm to bring back in time the essence of Civil's grandmother. As she washes her hands with rum, the audience starts coming in one by one. Slowly, she performs the ritual with coffee beans and music, memories and pictures unveiling an identity with Haitian roots. With these actions, presence is (re) semantized and obtains a different value. It is about the need to belong, identity; the importance of having an origin and a meaning of life.

The body will always be a space of revision; it is a stage, a courtyard. It is where hundreds of situations—public and private—come across doubts and thoughts to be questioned, unfolded and unveiled.

# Muño ( fantasía de la negrita )

( distillation / threshold / new moon ritual )
at the entrance, i stand in an elastic black dress
conforming to my body, a purple straw basket of treasures
and a silver basin at my feet

> from the basket, i pull out a brand new bottle
> of negrita rum: transparent, white
>> in the background, these songs:
>> "shirk" —meshell ndegéocello
>> "you go to my head" —billie holiday
>> "i know who you are" —björk

muñeca –    1. parte del cuerpo humano.
            2. juguete en forma de figura de mujer o de niña

muñir –     convocar a una junta u otro acto semejante
            *sin.* amañar, manejar, preparar, disponer,
            manipular, arreglar, apañar
            (*diccionario de la lengua española*)

translation:    to summon, call, convoke
                (*cassell's spanish–english dictionary*)

*muño*          *muñeca*         *moon*          *yo*

I summon – I call – I convoke

> i open the bottle and pour a libation to the ancestors
> i move the bottle in the air to the four corners
> i cup my right hand and pour rum into it and drink
> i cup my left hand and pour rum and let it fall into the basin
> i set down the bottle and rub my rum-washed hands together
> i summon the public
> i take each person, cup their hands, and pour rum into them
>> they can drink it or let it fall
>> they enter the space

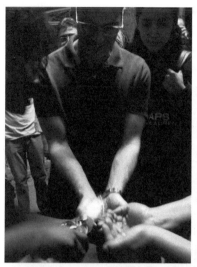

( invocation )
black out. lights up.
i walk from the doorway to the stage
        the purple straw basket on my arm
        the silver basin on my head
i am singing a song from my maternal grandmother
        "jesus loves me this I know"
if the rum ritual was haiti, this song is african-america
        both my legacy
i stop on stage, set down the basin and the basket
        pour more rum into the basin
i open another bottle of rum, salute the four corners
        and begin to pour again

instead of white rum, black Mexican coffee emerges
its smell mingles with the smell of the rum
a projection of the negrita brand rum label appears behind me
i make a magic circle of coffee around the silver basin of rum
i speak in Spanish—part memorized lines, part improvisation
      aquí está Performagia      here is Performagia
        magia             magic
      yo soy magia         I am magic
      la gente me dice que soy magia     people tell me I'm magic
      yo soy negra         I am a black woman
      magia negra         black magic woman

    I dance on the wide circle of coffee grounds,
        slip sliding, intoning in my strange Spanish
  Estaba buscando mi abuelita
      I was looking for my grandmother
Estaba buscando mi abuelitita
        I was looking for my grand-grandmother
Estaba buscando mi abuelita / y ya no está
      I was looking for my grandmother / she's not there

Estaba buscando mi abuelita
        I was looking for my grandmother . . . .
                en el DF
                en Veracruz
                en Oaxaca
                en Tijuana
                a la frontera
                en Tlaxcala
                en la luna
                en la tierra

        Estaba buscando mi abuelita
        I was looking for my grandmother
            y ya no está
            she's not there
        En lugar, yo encontré la Negrita
        instead, I found the Negrita

( transformation )
the projection changes to *"muño (fantasía de la negrita)"*
from the purple basket comes an old-fashioned tape recorder
i press play and you hear my voice
reading a cut-up of the following texts:
"la mujer negra" —nancy morejón
"egotripping" —nikki giovanni
"femme nue, femme noire" —léopold sédar senghor
"who's afraid of aunt jemima" —faith ringgold
"phenomenal woman" —maya angelou
+ lines from my curriculum vitae

*e.g. à l'ombre de ta chevelure / Phenomenal woman / Todavía
huelo la espuma del mar que me hicieron atravesar / Anacaona
/ I am a gazelle so swift / It's in the reach of my arms / La noche
no puedo recordarla / with a packet of goat's meat / Concentration
in Comparative Literature (High Honors) / Bajo su sel sembré,
recolecté y las cosechas no comí. / the span of my hips, / "whisper
(the index of suns" / traídos a ella, o no igual que yo." etc. etc. etc.*
a collision of heritage, a chrysalis of identity

while this plays, i take off the elastic black dress, show skin
i pull from the purple basket, la Negrita's dress
i let it stand on its own crinoline for a minute
before slowly putting it on
i zip myself up from the back
i pull out her shoes one by one, bend over, and put them on
i shake out two scarves and tie them together on my head
with deliberation, i find myself in her body,
or rather, my body in her
i outstretch my hands and close them into fists
i discover myself

# < la negrita ya está >

the projection changes again
to a series of slides of la negrita doll in the world.
la negrita at the parque mexico in el distrito federal
at a newsstand wearing a cubraboca. in a french bakery
in tlaxcala in front of the cathedral

        The chilena song "el negro de la costa"
        by pepe ramos begins to play

la Negrita does a happy doll dance!
la Negrita lays in wait!
la Negrita gives hugs!
(la Negrita takes care of the chirren!)
la Negrita hunts for food!
la Negrita considers the Negrito in her pocket!
will she eat it, indulge her cannibal tendencies?
( . . . it's not enough—it's not enough . . . )
la Negrita encounters / reenters the sacred circle

      estaba buscando mi abuelita
    I was looking for my grandmother
      mi abuelitititi teeeeeeeth
    my gran gran gran motheeth
       teeeeeeeth

| | |
|---|---|
| estaba buscando | I was looking |
| estaba buscando | I was looking |
| estuve buscando | I did looking |
| estoy buscando | I am looking |

    yo busco mi abuelita la negrito
    I look for my grandmother the negrita
      una negrita, muñequita,
    a negrita, a little doll (with moon)

pero yo encontré
but I found
muñequita, moooooooooo
a little moon doll, mooooooooooon
yo encontré la muñequita, la negrita
I found my little doll, a negrita
yo muño
I summon—I convoke—I call
mi abuelita la negrita y yo
my grandmother la negrita and me

i pick up the silver basin and pour the rum over my head
it falls over my body, over my costume, seeps into my skin
i place the empty silver basin over my head
i outstretch my arms, close my hands to fists.

[*FIN*]

* * *

June 10, 2009

So so so so so so so so so so much has happened since I've last
written in this notebook. All of Tlaxcala, Performagia, treated like a rock
star, dealing with disorganization, professing my truths as a performance
artist, leading a taller, encountering the refined taste of fresh pulque,
the press/mess of a beautiful man's tattooed fingers, the feel of his
collarbone and from the bottom to the top, naming each part in Spanish:
uñas, dedos, pies, piernas, pene, estomago, pecho, brazo, uñas, manos,
hombros, cuello, barba, boca, labios, nariz, ojos – oh and what I still
forget: eyebrows – frente, cabello – to be kissed, to be seen – to be seen
by the whole town – dancing in <u>the tigre</u> – vocalizing in the morning –
feeling, being beautiful, In the hour between waking and leaving E.'s
room on Sunday morning, I think fucking me awed, tired him out a little
(. . . DEMONIOS he said in bed with me)

# I am
# cracking
# into bloom

* * *

Last night I was thinking about the fact that C. hadn't been in touch for
a whole week – never texted me or called to wish me luck on the show.
I felt caught in a venus fly trap – wanting to reach out to him only to tell
him, confirm that we're both completely free. And I don't need to tell
him about E. – chamaco, no vaquero, sexando con botes, tatuajes, 666,
pompadour, moist lips, aviator shades, kung fu massive cross in his
house – and how I couldn't just slip off and be in my own bed. The whole
breakfast table looking at me "Que hiciste anoche Gabrielle? we all saw
you go off with that man" asked Laura G, – whom I really like. And my
answer – "Lo que pasa en Tlaxcala, se queda en Tlaxcala." And everyone
roared with laughter.

And I felt very much like a beautiful rock star – and then needing to
return to the routine of real life – I don't feel guilty relative to C. But as

188

Yolaine said – it's murky. I don't want to be dishonest, but I also don't need to go out my way to flaunt my dalliances with other men. But the things he's said to me are so confusing "What do you want Gabrielle – in your life?" "To make art, teach, do good in the community." "So you don't want a family?" "No, I'd like a family. . . but that may not happen." "What do you mean?" "No man has ever told me that he loved me." " What about you?" "You've never told me that you loved me." "A man would be scared to say that" – WAIT maybe it wasn't scared. Maybe it was just – "it would be hard for a man to say he was in love with you, since you are more about your career than love."

> I don't believe this is true.
> But I need to think more about it.
> I don't know what I said next.
> Other things I remember.
> Telling him
> I do belong to you.
> We have a connection,
> Telling him
> I do have love for you
> and him asking me
> how much.
> Him saying: I don't belong to you
> and you don't belong to me.
> Him saying: you're an alma libre.
> Him saying: the first time
> we had sex was horrible.
> Him telling me: that he knew
> he was sometimes cold.

And then last night realizing that I was really angry. That anger was finally the right place to go. That he wasn't treating me well. That he wasn't being kind enough, wasn't there for me when I needed him, didn't consistently check in, didn't reassure me or tell me that I was beautiful or good. That he criticized me then told me basically he was afraid I'd break his heart. That I know I'm not in love with him. But that maybe I could be – if he really opened himself to me – but maybe he's right – maybe I am too self-possessed. It was so good for E. to break into the dynamic. Although I do wonder if a person can feel more lonely after an affair.

No, that wasn't me. I felt really good yesterday until I got the email from Ex Teresa saying that they weren't gonna pay for a measly postcard for the show. And all my rock star swagger just smashed – and what hurt was I didn't feel connected enough to anyone here to just call and vent and be reassured. I feel lonely and disconnected and at times eager to leave. It's hard to speak another language all day. I can feel constantly underestimated as an artist and like I have to eat shit just to show my skills. But at the same time, I woke up this morning extra early, did art business, straightened the house, connected w/ Ex Teresa, talked to Madhu and my mother, and Dani P called for us to have coffee, and L. texted and wants to hang out (presumably to have sex) and I have a dinner tonight and a party and rehearsal tomorrow and I'd say this has been the best year of my life.

Te doy las gracias Virgencita de San Juan por la hermosa noche de
pasion que pase con Erwing Salamandra en Tlaxcala despues del
exito que tuve al presentar mi obra de Performançe Muño.
Nunca logramos ser en verdad una pareja pero aun asi nuestro
tiempo juntos fue inolvidable. 6 DE JUNIO DE 2009
GABRIELLE CIVIL

# EX VOTOS

*"Gracias Virjencita gracias a ti Jesus por el milagro
de haber ganado la beca Fulbright-Garcia Robles
para hacer el arte del Performance en Mexico . . ."*

Ex votos commemorate a moment of thanksgiving.
These small tin paintings represent an answered prayer. They depict a moment of delivery from disaster. A bullfighter who survived being gored by a bull, a person attacked by thieves, or a woman who endured grueling childbirth might all have an ex voto made. So might a black feminist performance artist rescued from the Great White North and allowed to come to Mexico. An ex voto (short for "ex voto suscepto" in Latin meaning "from the vow made") fulfills a vow of devotion after an experience of divine aid. In earlier centuries, ex votos lined the walls of many Catholic churches. Now you can find rows of ex votos at La Lagunilla, the best antique market in Mexico City. That's where I met Gustavo Villeda.

Trained as an engineer, Gustavo turned to dealing antiques after he got laid off from his job. He's a friendly guy, smart, thoughtful, and with a fantastic sense of humor. He has a knack for spotting compelling objects and an easy way with talking to shoppers. Original objects from previous centuries can fetch a pretty penny, but much of the antique market now consists of knock offs for tourists. Gustavo's ex votos feature everyone from hairdressers to street walkers to people miraculously revived from illness. I loved the vivid colors and outrageous situations. Obsessed with Haitian tourist art, I'm always interested in what gets constructed as authentic culture in a place, where and how the folkloric and commercial meet.

"Do you know where I can find an ex voto painter?" I asked Gustavo.

"I can do it for you," he replied. "I made a bunch of these."

"Ha! You mean the ones that say 1939 and 1947 were made by you?"

"Of course!" he answered laughing.

So we started to make ex votos together.

Gustavo had already worked with a German artist on an ex voto project, so he was ready to make it happen. When we talked about the price, neither one of us wheedled or haggled over money. He asked for what seemed to be a fair sum, and I paid him. He made and delivered the paintings as he said he would. The rights to the paintings would be mine, but I always make sure to include his name whenever I show them. Through a process of storytelling, discussion, art direction and production, we made the work together.

I was blessed to work with many Mexican artists, curators, musicians, and performers, but my collaboration with Gustavo was special. Our exchange was commercial and artistic, financial and personal, professional and social. Across the intersection of our various identities— Mexican and black American, older and younger, male and female, native and expatriate, ex voto painter and artistic believer, we had a wonderful time! Following the traditional process, we talked through my ex voto scenarios at length. Gustavo got a kick out of my adventures. Our first meetings were at La Lagunilla, then we met for lunch in town, and by the end, he was inviting me to his house for lunch with his wife and son.

The bottom of an ex voto always includes an inscription which gives thanks and explains the scene. Because traditional ex voto painters usually lacked formal education, the Spanish in the inscriptions would often be imperfect. Seen as part of the humble charm of the works, this aligned with my own unpolished tongue. (Errors remain inescapable in my Mexico / performance / writing.) And Gustavo made sure to slip in some errors in the ex voto inscriptions he painted for me.

Gustavo, a well-educated engineer and antiques dealer, was posing as an illiterate painter to render an image of authentic Mexican culture for an expatriate diasporic black feminist artist. Regard these ex votos as black feminist acts of trickster infiltration. Together, Gustavo and I shift form and slip into another landscape.

* * *

mid-May 2009

From the start of my Fulbright Fellowship in August 2008
this is what I've been working towards
the culmination
the finale
the big shebang and also my real
DF debut – my coming out party
my comment on my experiences here in Mexico
as well as a kind of retrospective showing/remix
of the work I've been making here so far.
I can't say I'm not scared or worried . . .

BUT I HAVE TO BELIEVE IN MYSELF

Here again – images – language – accumulation
but is there a central action –
will pace and overlap create the driving force
so the piece will feel energetic and not static –
to be inside the piece –
it also depends on the mariachis if they stay and how they could be better used
it's a fantasia – but also like a parade of images – but also a tour?
Through my experience – my year – or maybe more too like a pageant

* * *

May 21, 2009
exactly 4 weeks – before I premiere this finale show at Ex Teresa . . .
It's hard to peg exactly how I feel right now – disconnected, unprepared,
unimpressed with my own ideas, tired, gearing up, ready for people not to like
it, for a ho-hum response – or skirting away from the deep engagement that can
so easily lead to PAIN!

Does it ever feel better? Does the artist ever know how to do it? How to start?
. . . always, always that challenge, that thrill of LEARNING HOW TO WORK...

THIS IS IT!
If I came to Mexico to be a performance artist, I have been one.
If being a performance artist is about risking oneself, having ideas, making
them happen, social networking, a dose of humiliation, an engagement with the
public, an examination of the private, exterior acts as interior explanation –

I have learned this – am learning this – acting upon – enacting this this year and somehow that's what this final Fulbright piece is about...

> *dear saint theresa,*
> *dear little flower,*
> *we ask you saintly maid*
> *to shower blessings which you have*
> *promised to all who ask your aid*
> *and let them fall then a SHOWER*
> *of roses – sending blessings*
> *everywhere...*
> *dear saint theresa*
> *sweet child of jesus*
> *oh listen to our*
> *prayer*

So much unknowing. I don't know if it is the same St. Theresa or another one – and yet the grounding, the rooting for me in that song – a song that people won't know – a translation that people will still not understand how much is the attempt to translate ultimately an act of persistent ( further) mystery or mystification? . . . What does it mean that I still invest in writing (and reading) as a way to enter and engage performance?

\* \* \*

I'm working with Andrea's boyfriend Ponce on this show. Andrea, another one of Daniel's zillion friends in the city. After hanging out a bunch of times, he said YES to doing this with me. I feel so lucky. Ponce is dope! Here's to making the "net work" as sorors used to say. Friends of friends of friends. It's all about who you know. Now know thyself! I NEED TO TRUST MYSELF and also my instincts and find a way into/ to love what I make. I need to put these shows in my body.

There was something about how Molly and I worked in "How's Work" that is such a model for what I want to do/how I want to work with Ponce. We didn't write anything down. We did it – we came up with the concept, rehearsed once and then did it – and it was brilliant.

# PONCE PIRATA

apocalyptic visionary
you recall the smell
of the dead

bodies
in the trembling
centro

ten thousand strong
yourself not yet
born

as Apache-Pirata
wreck
age

you etch
patriotic haunting
global cleaving

intuiting renegade
scratch in
graphics

you carve names
into time
table

you enter stage right
a cosmogram
my brother

pour the rose petals
draw close and cosmic
move with me

# A DAY IN THE LIFE

L. contacted me out of the blue on Wed to hang out on Thursday. . . I had a huge day of rehearsal and then ran into Laura G. at the Spanish Cultural Center (and met Victoria C. whom I like) and some hot musicians . . . And then went to a Comexus cocktail party – where I set up plans to hang out with Will H (and that was fun – Ruta 61------> BLUES club!) But L. was supposed to contact me and never did. And I had my orange lingerie on and I was in a different space though after Tlaxcala, I didn't need L. to know I was beautiful and sexy and desirable and because of that I felt like I could hold back or rather than just being at his beck and call, I could be honest and tell the truth – and get into a mode where he would finally tell the truth. I wrote him a text that said "Qué pasó? ¿Es juego?" --- "Perdón corazón – work blah blah" and I said ----> why did you call me, I know you don't care about me, but wtf <---- or to that effect. And he said he really wanted to see me and could he come over. And I said "Ven – but I'm in an ornery mood." And he was like "Ornery – what does that mean?" And I said, "Come find out." And he said, "How about breakfast tomorrow" and I said – "what time? – I'll be there." So he kept me waiting for over 20 minutes and I'd sent him a text saying if he didn't arrive in 10 more minutes I would leave. And he came in – running, disheveled, not so handsome to me. Broad face – big ears, stubble. And we spoke in English and I told him. "Why did you call me this week but not before? Is it just when you want to have sex? When I really needed a friend and reached out to you, you weren't there. You call me exigente, but I haven't demanded anything from you." All in English over chilaquiles. He had steak and veggies or eggs or something. It wasn't all heated. We spoke of banal things – but it was the first time we'd hung out when we didn't have sex. And I felt both free of something but also hopeful that maybe we could be friends. Like I had come to a place where I would ask him for help and he'd do it. We talked about possibly getting together tonight – I'm on the fence. There's a cocktail party – and I'd like to go to dinner with Wendy and then drinks at Nick and Jim's. And I know L. doesn't drink and we're not that public. Plus there's E. That was an affair: we have no claim on each other. But should I just have sex with L. because I can, because touch would be reassuring? When I actually think about having sex with E. would that impact, dissipate my memory of him, or would it solidify something else. Yesterday C. called (and he'd texted right before) and I'm curious of course – but it's starting to matter to me less and less ------> I think it's good that I haven't gotten into it with him before the show – quiet time for focusing and it's hard for me to clarify exactly what I want to say/do except try to make "In an Out of Place."

June 2009

I feel a little like I'm drowning in time. It's dumb because there are things in my performance that certainly could use some work and there are key logistics – like the flower petals that aren't resolved – yet I want this show to happen. I want to do it, be ready and prepared for it, calm and in my body. Not harried like <u>Tie Air</u> - but I also still want to have adrenaline. A part of me has already moved on because I've been working on it so long – and I'm already feeling disconnected from the aftermath. Don't really want to talk or hang out with people here after the show. Don't want to drink mezcal. Wish E. could come. Don't want to smile or small talk.

\* \* \*

I'm so glad I brought Ralph Lemon's *Geography* here with me to Mexico. I've had the book for 4 ½ years and never read it – waiting for a time when I thought it would resonate. It's resonating now. Especially the anguish and agony Lemon feels about his work – his doubt, fear, self-recrimination.

He wrote, "Once a week I seem to hit these pockets where I begin to shut down even in the midst of revelations." Is it schadenfreude to feel relieved by this? (Or a kind of kinship?) I remember watching his dance at BAM in those uncomfy chairs and also meeting him in JFK and being touched and mildly surprised by his kindness.

\* \* \*

Wed 6/16
Yesterday was the first time I felt shitty about the show. Rehearsal was lousy. Tons of technical snafus - where's the cord? Wait, I need to program the lights. And in the middle of it, Gerardo the videographer came with questions and demands – Ponce was arriving at 1 PM and Gerardo came just as Ponce arrived and a hour was taken up negotiating with him and Edith, I was already exhausted – had run off tons of copies of what we were doing that no one looked at. Felt completely out of my body. Felt like the show sucked. Like I sucked. Like all my big ideas would look stupid and confused and that there was no emotional release or strain of wildness----> nothing new.

And Ponce was wonderful, comforting, present, funny although a bunch of stuff we still don't have down. There was a moment when I had to really release my ego because I was very annoyed that a curator from upstairs just waltzed in – after weeks of me working with Jorge and the production team and had tons of

201

opinions, etc. At the same time, she was right about mostly everything – so her opinion was valuable – It's a normal part of the process – esp. with work that's been going on so long – to feel shitty about work night before you do it. And I'm glad I read <u>Geography</u> in which Ralph Lemon felt shitty most of the time. This is that moment when you need reassurance – and at least I had Ponce. But I almost want to reach out to Lorena, Rosa, look at E.'s tattoos...

* * *

LOOSENESS
    PRESENCE
        IMPROVISATION

What <u>would</u> it mean to take more risks in the context of this show?
Does taking more risks take more time in preparation--->
and yet – I've been working on this show for a <u>YEAR</u>.
Really recognize that – claim it
all the things I've done this year all my experiences –
this is all part of it and is connected as such.
But I need to believe in it – see the show and own it

* * *

TODAY IS SHOW DAY
Some things I learned
*1) Everything takes more time than you think
*2) <u>No one</u> cares as much about your show as you do (so be organized, have your shit together and don't be surprised when you get pushed to the side – just stick up for yourself staying as dignified and gracious as you can)
3) Plan ahead <----- I've really done this. This is the first huge show I can think of when I feel like I have time to chill before getting ready . . . I zoned them out more or less but
4) I NEED QUIET
It's not that realistic in huge institutions with tech people and collaborators – but what I really need before a show—peace and quiet – no chattering or small talk
5) It's pivotal to stretch and be in the body beforehand
6) It's hard to direct yourself and perform
----> That disastrous Monday rehearsal was connected to that
7) Relationships are everything. I love the Chopo and El Museo de Arte de Tlaxcala. I love the tech guys at Ex Teresa – Jorge, Tonio, Carlos, Arturo, Chucho the sweeper – the guards – Celia, Juana, the guys – have all been great although I'm sad that upstairs they've not integrated me in the events of the year or "aprovechar"ed of my presence or expertise. . . I don't feel valued or valuable
----> even though it's undoubtedly true that they have done things for me – this show is happening (in 5 hours!) and they're letting me do it. But that sense --->

202

to be allowed to do it – instead of there being excitement about my work. I don't feel like they believe in me. Pancho López on the other hand, El Chopo. I'd do anything for/with them. It's probably best that E. isn't gonna be at the show ---->
C. and maybe L. – But I DO STILL WISH I HAD A HAND TO HOLD AFTER THE SHOW TONIGHT – <u>HIS HAND</u>!

I just have to hold the energy

# After Ten Months and Two Days in Mexico City – <u>TONIGHT</u> <u>IS</u> <u>THE</u> <u>SHOW</u>!

# Desde un costado de la caja
## Una reflexión en torno a dos obras de Gabrielle Civil
## por Pancho López

2

En sus visitas a México, Civil descubrió el imaginario popular de la ciudad, o buena parte del mismo. Cromos, revistas, mercados, fayuca, jugos, comida, color… un universo diferente al suyo, pero al mismo tiempo propio. Sin duda, lo que atrapó su atención fue el mariachi y sus rituales y no tardó en poner en marcha un plan para incorporarlos en su obra.

Entre rosas y luces, recuerdo en In & out of place esa silueta detallada, ataviada con un vestido largo, bailando al son del mariachi. Las sombras crecían y llenaban la sala del espacio empleado para el performance: Ex Teresa Arte Actual -quizá uno de los escenarios más importantes para el performance en toda América- y mientras Civil preparando un rezo, que le ayudara a entender su origen, que le ayudara a entenderse, que develara su pertenencia, su ubicación espacial, su persona, su ser. Masticar hielo es quizás como dar un beso. Y mientras los mariachis cantaban e inundaban con sus acordes el espacio, al igual que las sombras, ese espacio que en un tris tras de tan público se transforma en privado en el momento del beso, íntimo acto que siempre se vuelve el clímax esperado, el momento más acariciado que incluso raya en el cliché, pero que es tan honesto como preguntarse de dónde eres…

El amor tal vez sea un tema recurrente del humano, sentirse amado, cuestionarse real.
Las relaciones con las que uno se identifica son tan importantes como para desplazarse kilómetros, buscar el amor, la paz y la esencia de la vida. En eso pienso con la obra de Gabrielle Civil, que llena el espacio de color y de música.

Justo palabras como amor, color y música, son parte de la receta que uno encuentra a un costado de la caja, una mañana especial en la que uno se decide a prepararse unos hot cakes.

# From a Side of the Box
## An essay on two works by Gabrielle Civil
## by Pancho López
## translated by Lucía Abolafia Cobo

2

In her visits to Mexico, Civil discovered the popular imagery of the city—or a big chunk of it. Posters, magazines, markets, piracy, juices, food, colour . . . a universe different from hers, but at the same time her own. Undoubtedly, mariachis and their rituals caught her attention and soon enough she began a plan to integrate them into her work.

Among roses and lights, I remember in *In & Out of Place*, her detailed silhouette attired in a long dress and dancing to the Mariachi rhythm. Shadows arrived and filled the space of the room used for the performance at Ex Teresa Arte Actual—perhaps one of the most important spaces used for performance throughout America—as Civil prepared a prayer to help her understand her origin, to understand herself, to reveal her sense of belonging, spatial location, her persona, her being. To chew ice is perhaps how to give a kiss. As Mariachis sang and their chords flooded the public space—just as the shadows did—in just a second, such space turned into a private one that allowed a kiss. An intimate act always turns into an expected climax; a cherished moment that borders on cliché, but that is as honest as it is to wonder where you are from.

Love may be a reoccurring human topic; to feel loved and to question existence. The relationships that we identified with are important enough to make us travel many kilometers to seek love, peace and the essence of life. I think about that when Gabrielle Civil's work fills the space with color and music.

It is precisely with words like love, color, and music that the recipe can be found on the side of the box like on a special morning when you decide to make yourself some pancakes.

# IN & OUT OF PLACE (MÉXICO, DF)

More than any of the other performances I made that year, "In & Out of Place (México, DF)" is the hardest to describe. It was fantasia, dreamscape, extravaganza. It had the largest venue, involved the most collaborators, and drew the largest audience (it felt like hundreds of people). It was overflowing with ideas. In this work, I was trying to synthesize all the different kinds of feelings and experiences that I had in Mexico. On stage, I wanted to be the foreigner, the clueless gringa, the full-bodied lover, and glamorous performance artist all at once. I wanted to reflect the world around me. Both synthesis and dissonance.

Along with the Mariachis México Internacional who had performed with me near the US Embassy, I also invited Rodrigo Betancourt Ponce, a talented graphic artist and member of Daniel's inner circle, to perform with me at Museo Ex Teresa Arte Actual. Because so much of my year had been about navigating Mexican masculinity, it felt important to bring that energy directly on the stage. I also wanted to show things usually out of place. This included: snow, ice, my black female body, mariachis playing and singing jazz, and cheers for loneliness.

At my elementary school, Shrine of the Little Flower, we used to sing a song to Saint Theresa and I was struck by that coincidence. I knew I wanted to bring that Detroit area Saint Theresa, that memory of little Gabby Civil into this place, Ex Teresa, even if no one else would recognize the reference. I wanted to bring the chorus of the song to life where "a shower of roses" falls like blessings in the air.

I was also thinking about the inner workings of the museum which were usually out of view. During rehearsals, I got friendly with technical and custodial staff. I had the idea of asking Juana, one of the museum's caretakers, to be a part of the show. No one had ever invited her to be in a performance before and she was really excited.

At the top of the show, Juana and the mariachis welcomed the audience while I was not there in person, literally out of place. Later, Juana came sweeping and swirling rose petals while Ponce and I danced down the aisle, a reminder of the people in Ex Teresa who cared for the floors, the walls, the lights, and the sound. I couldn't have made the show without them.

In & Out of Place (Mexico DF)

performed at Museo Ex Teresa Arte Actual

June 13, 2009

\*

Walk into the museum from the outside

See projected in the vestibule an ex voto of me

getting the good news about the Fulbright

Mariachis arrive and begin to play

"Lift Ev'ry Voice and Sing" in English

(The Negro National Anthem)

As they sing, Juana a Caretaker of the museum

comes and sweeps around them

I am spectral in the other room

The audience files in to see me

Over the mainstage

*Yawo's Dream* begins to play

In this video, I take off my winter clothes

in Minnesota and end up barefoot in snow

in a yellow dress

throwing flowers in the river

Three minutes later, the Mariachis arrive

to play a fanfare for my arrival

I make my entrance from the back door

in a red dress. Once I'm there,

the Mariachis bow and leave the stage

I sing a prayer to Saint Theresa

that I learned in grammar school

*

I pull out a tape recorder and press play

Amplified, you hear my voice

reading "the African woman"

section of *Heart of Darkness*

in a funny British accent

Ponce the Translator reads the Spanish

translation

into a microphone

I do a dance

with a banana

to these mingling voices

I must eat the banana

because at the end of the dance

I slip on the banana peel

*

# SCORE FOR BANANA DANCE

"Dark human shapes could be made out in the distance, flitting indistinctly against the gloomy border

"Formas humanas oscuras podrían ser hechas fuera a lo lejos, revoloteando indistintamente contra

of the forest, and near the river two bronze figures, leaning on tall spears, stood in the sunlight under

la frontera oscura del bosque, y cerca del río dos figuras de bronce, inclinándose en lanzas altas, se

fantastic headdresses of spotted skins, warlike and still in statuesque repose. And from right to left

pararon en la luz del sol bajo tocados fantásticos de pieles con motas, belicoso y todavía en reposo

along the lighted shore moved a wild and gorgeous apparition of a woman.

escultural. Y del derecho de dejar por la costa iluminada movió una tierra virgen y aparición

She walked with measured steps, draped in striped and fringed cloths, treading the earth

magnífica de una mujer. Ella anduvo con pasos medidos, drapeado a rayas y telas deshilachadas,

proudly, with a slight jingle and flash of barbarous ornaments. She carried her head high; her hair

pisando la tierra orgullosamente, con un tintineo y el destello leves de ornamentos bárbaros. Ella

was done in the shape of a helmet; she had brass leggings to the knee, brass wire gauntlets to the

llevó la cabeza alta; el pelo fue hecho en forma de un casco; ella tuvo polainas de latón a la rodilla,

elbow, a crimson spot on her tawny cheek, innumerable necklaces of glass beads on her neck;

guanteletes de alambre de latón al codo, un lugar carmesí en la mejilla leonado, collares

bizarre things, charms, gifts of witch-men, that hung about her, glittered and trembled at every

innumerables de cuentas de vidrio en el cuello; cosas extrañas, los encantos, los regalos de bruja-

step. She must have had the value of several elephant tusks upon her. She was savage and superb,

hombres, eso colgó acerca de ella, brilló y tembló en cada paso. Ella debe haber tenido el valor de

wild-eyed and magnificent; there was something ominous and stately in her deliberate progress.

varios colmillos de elefante sobre ella. Ella fue salvaje y magnífica, de mirada salvaje y magnífica;

And in the hush that had fallen suddenly upon the whole sorrowful land, the immense wilderness,

había algo siniestro y majestuoso en su progreso deliberado. Y en la quietud que se había caído de

the colossal body of the fecund and mysterious life seemed to look at her, pensive, as though it had

repente sobre la tierra dolorosa entera, el desierto inmenso, el cuerpo colosal de la vida fecunda y

been looking at the image of its own tenebrous and passionate soul. She came abreast of the

misteriosa pareció mirarla, pensativo, como si había estado mirando la imagen de su propia, el alma

steamer, stood still, and faced us. Her long shadow fell to the water's edge. Her face had a tragic

tenebrosa y apasionada. Ella vino parejo del barco de vapor, se paró todavía, y nos encaró.

and fierce aspect of wild sorrow and of dumb pain mingled with the fear of some struggling, half-

Ella ensombrece mucho tiempo se cayó a la orilla del agua. La cara tuvo un aspecto trágico y violento de

shaped resolve. She stood looking at us without a stir and like the wilderness itself, with an air of

pena salvaje y de dolor mudo mezclado con el temor de algún luchar, resolución de mitad-formó. Ella se

brooding over an inscrutable purpose. A whole minute passed, and then she made a step forward.

paró nos mirando sin una conmoción y como el desierto mismo, con un aire de empollar sobre un propósito

inescrutable. Un minuto entero pasó, y entonces ella hizo a un delantero de paso.

There was a low jingle, a glint of yellow metal, a sway of fringed draperies,

Había un tintineo bajo, un destello de metal amarillo, un vaivén de colgaduras deshilachadas,

and she stopped as if her heart had failed her."

y ella pararon como si el corazón la hubiera fallado."

— Joseph Conrad, Heart of Darkness / El corazón de las tinieblas

211

Ponce the Local comes and helps me up.

"Hola" he says / "Hello" I say

"Buenas Noches" / "Good Evening"

"¿De Dónde Eres?"

He asks and then asks again

"¿De Dónde Eres?"

"¿De Dónde Eres?"

and we begin a language duet

"¿De Dónde Eres?" where I answer

politely at first "¿De Dónde Eres?"

then more and more absurdly

with language and with body

"¿De Dónde Eres?"

I sing an old song

from a McDonald's commercial

*you - deserve - a - break - today*

"¿De Dónde Eres?"

Near the end of our volley

I grab a big bag of ice

and spread it across the stage

"¿De Dónde Eres?"

I try to use this to explain

and end up grabbing

a handful of ice and eating it

slowly in real time

"¿De Dónde Eres?" fades out

I am from Iceland

I stand on the stage

in silence eating ice cubes

*

Ponce the Fotógrafo snaps a picture of me

He takes pictures from different angles

Knowing that it's what they want

I invite the audience to take pictures of me too

They take many pictures on their phones

*

The Mariachis return and begin to play "Bésame Mucho"

Ponce the Lover and I move close and start to kiss

*Tie Air Kiss* begins to play behind us

L. and I are French kissing and playing with tongues


Then I read a spurned woman letter I wrote to L.

Ponce interprets it in real time

*Dear L—*
*Thank you very much for your massage a few weeks ago.*
*Who keeps baby oil in the kitchen? Handy.*
*Forgive my writing in English.*
*Surely an enterprising young man such*
*as yourself can find a way to translate.*
*In the meantime, Spanish is starting to seep into me.*
*Chicharrones. Lluvia. Fotos sin aretes.*
*Everything turns into art one way or another.*
*Even you. Don't worry—Glenn Close was a blond*
*white woman in Fatal Attraction. Black women have more pride.*
*Usually. My problem is that I hate loose ends. So.*
*Adios. Go Pistons! I wish I had taken a picture of your shoes.*
*Gabrielle*

*

Do I really open a package of Negritos

and eat them on the stage?

¡Antropofagia! ¡Riquísimo!

*

I take off my red dress

and put on a big red ball gown

Ponce the Chambelán zips me up the back

The Mariachis return to play

"Feeling Good"

or something brassy

# In & Out of Place – Gabrielle Civil     CUE SHEET

| Gabrielle | Ponce | Cue |
|---|---|---|

Invocation

| | | |
|---|---|---|
| St. Theresa Canto | sings | throws petals from pockets |
| "to all who ask their aid" | moves white cube | after Gabrielle leaves |
| | | |
| Banana Dance | dances | reads from *Corazón de las Tinieblas* |
| after the fanfare | when the taperecorder turns on | |
| | | picks me up off the floor, twirl |
| Translator Intro | hola, etc.     hola, etc. | scream |
| | | |
| ¿De Dónde Eres? | body, language, song | *¿De Dónde Eres?* repetition |
| after the McDonald's song | | 2 more *¿De Dónde Eres?* |
| | | then BIENVENIDOS |

| | | |
|---|---|---|
| La Negra Duet/ Foto Shoot | *fake dance* | *laugh / cry* |
| | *aiming* | *Gab gets lifted / fish dance* |
| | *spin / binoculars* | *kidnap* |
| | *showing Gab to audience* | *fake dance* |
| | *tongues out* | *photo* |
| | | |
| Iceland | eats ice | slams bag on the floor |
| | | |
| Bésame Mucho/ Tracery | | slow dance/ trace each other |
| | | |
| Letter/ Negrito | reads letter | translates normally |
| at A MANO whips out Negrito | | |
| then only "everything turns into art" | | |
| my problem is I hate loose ends" | | |
| | | |
| Feelin' Good/ Petal Fall | changes into big red dress | moves cube |
| we both play, dance in the flowers | | ---->Juana comes |
| spreads petals     into the aisle/ audience | | puts them in my dress return to the cube |
| | | |
| ¡Viva Viva! | | throws petals on me, walks away |

218

Ponce and I grab big bags

    of yellow rose petals

        from the side of the stage

    We play in the petals

We spread petals down the aisle

    into the audience

    We dance

Juana returns and sweeps and swirls

    the petals around us

    Ponce and I return to the stage

*

¡VIVA MEXICO! I CALL ¡VIVA!

¡VIVA MEXICO! THE AUDIENCE RESPONDS

¡VIVA SOLEDAD! I CRY! THEY GASP & GROAN!

¡¡NOOO!! ¡VIVA DOLOR! ¡VIVA CAMBIO!

I CRY OUT A SERIES OF MEMORIES AND SENSATIONS

¡VIVA VIVA! ¡VIVA VIVA! ¡VIVA VIVA!

IT ENDS IN A SHOWER OF PETALS

# Comunión en Ex Teresa
## por Sergio Peña

Otra vez una canción típicamente norteamericana en versión mariachi en el marco de una ex iglesia colonial mexicana, cuyas amplias naves reproducen el eco de la melodía. El piso está cubierto de flores mientras la gente, ocupando lugares en dos hileras de bancas a modo de fieles en la iglesia, observa a la artista, mientras ella realiza una danza sensual, recorriendo el centro de la nave, y recoge flores que va arrojando al público mientras se dirige a un altar dónde toma su lugar frente al micrófono. Ahí la aguarda un colaborador para que juntos puedan dar inicio a una lectura vertiginosa, mientras una pantalla de video por detrás de ellos muestra imágenes de una pareja (¿ellos mismos?) besándose con pasión; voces de hombre y de mujer alternándose con la misma intensidad desbordada de la pareja besándose en el video; y esa escena tiene un efecto algo religioso para todos los que estamos ahí observando, no sólo por estar en un templo antiguo, sino porque lo que presenciamos tiene que ver con la idea de "comunión."

# Communion at Ex Teresa
## by Sergio Peña
## Translated by Lucía Abolafia Cobo

Once again, a typical American song in its Mariachi version was played in the context of what used to be a Mexican colonial church, whose big naves reproduced the echo of the melody. The floor was covered with flowers while people occupied two rows of benches as believers do in a church. The people observe the artist as she sensually dances along the center of the nave and picks up flowers that she throws to the audience on her way to an altar, where she takes her place in front of a microphone. There, a collaborator awaits her so that together they can begin a frenzied reading. A video screen behind them shows images of a couple (themselves?) passionately kissing. There are male and female voices that alternate with each other with the same overwhelmingly intensity as that of the couple kissing in the video. Such a scene has a somewhat religious effect for everyone here observing, not just because we are in an old temple, but because what we are witnessing has to do with the idea of "communion."

# June 19, 2009
# I DID THE
# SHOW!!!

All of yesterday, I was walking around thinking today is the day! Today I'm going to have my show! And when I arrived in the space (almost 5:45) I felt good and ready. I deposited things in our camarino – organized the petals – sang along with Meredith Monk – set up the computer with the projection, Ponce arrived, we organized our things. We breathed on the floor, we stretched to Vamos a la Playa (Cibo Matto). We danced to Let's Work (Prince). We did yoga. We set all the props. Tested the mike levels. I felt calm and ready. Someone from LIMBA - the big arts council did an interview with me before the show. I dolled myself up. Did a shot of tequila with Ponce and then stood on the white square.

> And the show began.
> It was a good one.
> It was good.
> I was good.

I like that the show was good hearted, light-hearted – well no – more like humorous but hit different tones. I liked that it moved from the past through different images – scenes – vignettes of Mexico – I added some things – clapping after the mariachis and before the video. I liked the banana dance. I liked making the crowd clap for us. . . .And I liked the feel of the petals in my hands. And their smell! Divine – and the mariachis were singing Nina Simone. And Ponce and I were playing with the petals and it was changing the energy of the space (we should have consolidated one last bag because there was a bag left we didn't use I would have loved even <u>more</u> petals on the ground – in the air.) And then Ponce was throwing flowers on me – and it was beautiful.

And I started with the <u>vivas</u> – and here's where I learned something. I should have probably gone from light to dark. I had them saying viva with me for the first few (I could also have made it more abstract – and just vivas – like a floating signifier)
But I liked switching it up –

having strange words that came in the moment.
But it was funny and maybe it was good --->
because I was like
VIVA crowd VIVA
me VIVA crowd <u>VIVA</u>
me VIVA dolor crowd what?!
But when I said viva tacos al pastor - the crowd went wild -
So next time – think about stoking them up – leading them through
positive ones and then switching the tone and getting darker from there
And also trying to have those last vivas – <u>hit more of the putazo</u>
Still with all that said, all in all I was grounded, clear, calm, and I
wouldn't believe how QUICKLY the show went. It felt like it flew by. But
I didn't feel like I rushed through it.
I like how the ice slowed me down. I liked my sassy moments with the
crowd in the photo shoot. I liked the feel of the petals on my skin. I liked
the loopiness of ¿de dónde eres? I liked when I rearranged my dress in
the viva and said ¡viva vestidos!

I wish there could have been more video – or a live feed of Ponce's
camera – But all in all, it was a well-realized, theatrical, non-linear, poetic
work. I don't know if it cracked open into a kind of wild emotional storm
the way *Tie Air* did. I wasn't taking the same kind of risks. But it was a
show that required skill, vision, imagination, and strong communication
and leadership skills – to arrange, explain, bring people together, get over
my own ego at times --->

Maybe that's the true strength of In and Out of Place, growing as a
<u>director</u>. As well as a performer, trusting myself. Building sequences,
spaces. It will be interesting (eventually) to see a videotape. I want to look
at my lighting, staging choices...

I can't believe it's over!
I can't believe I did the show!
I need to let myself be in the afterglow.
It was good! I was good! It was a success...

And after it was over, I felt really calm. I didn't feel devastated or
euphoric, I felt ---> wait is it over? Not anti-climactic (which is often a
form of sadness) but just clear. A little strange. Like I walked momentarily
through another world. I gave my gifts and payments to everyone. I
would have liked a big moment together, really wanted to get a picture

with Juana and her family ---> but it didn't happen that way.

Right after the show, Ponce and I were smoking and catching our breath
(paradoxical I know) and Anita and Jennifer and Cristobal and George F
came back. They brought me a sandwich and chips and good wishes.
And Anita brought me a boa.
And I changed into my white dress,
And I looked and felt beautiful.
But also slightly at a remove.

Did something happen in the show?
Did I make something happen?
Did something happen in me?
There'd been a show. It had come off.
People liked it. It was well done.
Was it good? Was it memorable?
Had it pushed something in me?
I felt today, just one day later,
still feel RELIEF
that it's over.
That I did it.
That I showed what I could do –
at least some of it.

Juarena, the head of the museum, came back to congratulate me.
He said he loved the show. And I thanked him profusely
and told him that it had been my dream to do a show at Ex Teresa and he
had helped make my dreams come true. Anytime he said, we're here for
you –
Vamos a ver...

I took the time to organize things in the dressing room.
Then it started to rain.
I walked out and all of the people were gone.
I was tempted to go home because I was tired and how to describe it . . .
I felt a little dazed, amazed, clear
but like a glass that had been emptied out.
I couldn't believe – from throngs to just me and Ponce on the street and
Calle Moneda was beautiful and empty. Kind of like that Paul Blackburn
poem –
("the lights, the lights, the fucking lights of Bklyn")

Then sheets of rain
Ponce was teaching me different Mexican words for rain –
I don't remember what they are – one for a cloudburst,
one for a heavy rain, one for a long lasting storm.
         What happened next was a poem
A man approached.
He was nicely dressed and had a backpack.
I didn't realize at first that he'd been to the show, but he had.
He asked me "¿de dónde eres?" as a joke.
We waited out the storm.
"Would you all like some vino tinto?"
At first, I didn't understand.
How could he have red wine? Was he asking us for wine?
For money to get wine? No – he had a brand new bottle of wine
and a corkscrew.
He uncorked it and we all took a drink.
It was from Spain and warmed the cockles of me.
Ponce had one more traje (a drag no – like from a cigarette)
and then the rain was subsiding.
It had been out of control hard and steady
but was calming down and I was walking to the curb to call a taxi and

the man said hey and I turned back to see him
and then he threw a handful of petals
from the show right on me.
The hard, yellow surprise,
the slap of the petals felt like fingertips.
What magic –

         He told us his name – Hector? Victor? But I couldn't quite catch
it. And it was such a strange encounter. Usually, I would get his name
and info or at least give him a card. But it was just a magical, mysterious
– beautiful moment with Ponce and this man in the rain right after the
show in the wet, glistening Zócalo.

And we were all there! Anita, her friend Gloria the b-day girl, Laura and Pedro, Will and Damian, Jennifer, George, Wendy, Aleida and her pals. I was arriving late! But they bought me beers – and we all laughed and chatted. And I had tacos from a place I'd gone to in Sept. with Jennifer when we left Daniel H's party where I met Franc C and tried to go to the Salon Corona but walked the wrong way. And there was some police scuffle that night and I'd only been in town a month. And it felt right 9 months later – to be at the Tlaquepaque next to that taco stand. After my show.

Wait – I have to write more about Ponce. How happy he was after the show. How many times he thanked me for being a part of it ---> for inviting him to be a part of it. How his <u>parents came</u>! How they liked the show. How he felt euphoria in his body, adrenaline, how he said his legs were weak by the end. How much he liked it. I'm so happy he had a good time. I'm so happy I invited him and he did it! And no matter what else, rather along with everything else – that last moment in <u>the rain was lovely.</u>

# DEAD LETTER OFFICE

Dear C.,

　　Thank you so much for coming to my show. I know you were working and it meant a lot to me that you came and that you liked it. I wish you could have stayed a little while after – at least to say hello to me. You're always talking about me leaving, but really, it's you who leaves me. I see you, we have a nice time and then I never know when I'll see or hear from you again. The last time I saw you was June 3 – I sent you a text that morning. Did you get it? It doesn't matter. Even if you didn't, I would have thought you might communicate with me. You told me the thing that bothered you most about your ex was the fact that she wasn't honest with you. So I'm going to be honest.

　　It hurt my feelings that you didn't call, text or write me for 2 weeks after sleeping with me in my bed, fighting mosquitos with me and hearing me tell you that I had love in my heart for you. Was this a kind of punishment? Or are you just that busy?

　　Before my show in Tlaxcala, friends from around the world wished me luck. From Mexico, the US, even Africa. Texts, Emails, calls. Not a word from you. I was disappointed, But then realized something. You were right, I am a free spirit. I won't be in Mexico forever. And the key for me is to aprovechar my time here. I care about you and have wanted to be your friend – but our dynamic hasn't been so great.

　　Sometimes I feel close to you and other times great distance. In the distance, when you're gone from me, I often need support or help – during the swine flu, before the show – and you're not there! You say I think my career is more important, but you often put your work ahead of me. And I understand that. But I want to be clear with you. We are/ have been connected, but we're both free. And in the time and space when you're gone, I'm making other connections, other men ask me out and I go. I'm writing this to you because I want to be honest and clear. I know you don't like my letters so I'll be short. I'm writing because I'm leaving town for 3 weeks and I don't want to leave without having things square with you.

```
Thanks for all you've brought to my life.
                     OR MAYBE
I do believe there's some reason why we know each other/were
brought together - so hopefully we can end my time in Mexico
on a good note.
          Enjoy Summer,
     and thank you for everything
          Gabrielle
```

I doubt I'll send this letter - This is the trick of affairs. Knowing how to keep quiet,
claim your own distance, be open and respectful, honoring the moment – but stay
clear, independent and light – remember - I can do whatever I want.

# WHAT I'VE LEARNED ABOUT MYSELF IN MEXICO CITY BY GABRIELLE CIVIL
### *(from my notebooks)*

- I like a tidy house and will take time and spend money to keep it that way.
- I've loved this apartment and had a chance to live in a way I probably couldn't afford in the US and it was worth spending more money to live well.
- I am preoccupied by ways to live, the impact of spaces on peace, happiness & productivity.
- Order matters much to me in a living /work space.
- An emptier room can be filled with presence, breath, creative action—like when I moved out most of the furniture in my living room and turned it into a yoga/ dance/ meditation / rehearsal space. I had never used my living room more or enjoyed it so much. Something to remember!
- I am disciplined and can set goals and meet them.
- I can make opportunities for myself (Obsidian Arts show, Tec classroom visit).
- I can work independently as an artist.
- I need other people, other eyes to make art.
- I don't like know-it-alls.
- Men do find me attractive (even when I don't always find myself so).
- Porn is instructive for showing what men want, expect, how to do things.
- If I have cigarettes, I smoke them.
- I smoke cigarettes as a personal ritual, a way of feeling my body.
- I need to stop smoking cigarettes out of boredom.
- I am easily bored.
- I like, need, and struggle with being alone.
  (This has been true of me since I was 20—maybe forever? Andover, NY? But here, I've learned this about myself, felt, seen, recognized it deeper ways.)
- I would rather be alone than with people I don't really like.
- I appreciate solitude but have a hard time relaxing—doing nothing . . .
- I can best do nothing lying on a wood floor in front of a sun-filled window.
- I'm looking for my own home, a place to be myself fully, happily with absorption. Mexico City is a great place, but it isn't it.
- I can't imagine living long term in a place where 1) I can't get my hair done 2) I can't routinely shop and buy great clothes and 3) I am constantly being asked where I'm from

- I'm good at living in / looking ahead to and for the future—here I've been much more in this present. The necessities of setting up and settling into a life in another country have forced me to be this way. This is good.
- I'm not so hot at relationships with men but I've gotten better.
- I've learned how to have sex with men. Or should I say I've improved...
- I've learned that sex matters a lot to me after the sexual death / deprivation of Minnesota but isn't the answer, doesn't replace kindness or connection.
- I'm ambivalent about connection.
- So far, I think I've preferred the idea of companionship (or what I wrote as Freudian slip in my journal as "compassionship") to the idea of intimacy. But maybe this also depends on the person and not just my desire/ need/ habit of self possession. Or maybe I'm deluded.
- I've learned that I'm pretty easy—sexually that is.
- I've learned that I actually like the missionary position. I like deep tongued kisses during the act. And I feel ambivalent about sex from behind. It can feel good, but I wonder about the lost connection when you can't see the other person's face. Have I just become an object? Or do I just not trust my partners? And on top, you have to work so hard!
- I've learned that I can have my worst fear come true (that a man would tell me that I'm a cold fish, have no chemistry, am bad at sex, don't know how to fuck) and it won't destroy me. Will come as a relief actually because the shoe has finally dropped and I can move on.
- I've learned that I'm tougher than I thought I was.
- I've learned that I'm pretty sensitive, but it can take me awhile to react to a slight.
- I've learned that I'm pretty forgiving but can hold grudges.
- I've learned that I'm withholding to people I don't completely trust.
- I've learned that I can be a punisher—use withholding as a means of revenge. Not good.
- I realize that language is key to my sense of self and intimacy with others. Daniel H told me that when things get deep with his boyfriend he speaks to him in English. I realize that it's hard for me to imagine being fundamentally deep with a person in another language. This is a crazy thought to have considering my parents are from two different countries and don't share the same first language and don't share more than one language at all. I wonder how my parents managed / have managed for so long with 2 different root languages. Does my father still think of English as alien? Is he another person in Kreyòl?
- I'm another person in Spanish.
- I'm another person in Mexico. (This is both good and bad.)
- I've learned that I value convenience, comfort and routine.

- I've learned I'm not particularly adventurous.
- I've learned how much I like linen, fluffy towels and good, clean sheets.
- I've learned that I have a *deep* relationship to laundry and that I will spend a lot of money doing it.
- I've learned that I hate dealing with the trash.
- I've learned that a key to life is managing expectations.
- Managing expectations does not / should not mean assuming you can't get what you want.
- Sometimes I'm a pessimist (Rosa told me a few months ago: "I wouldn't say you're optimistic, Gabrielle. You have a positive disposition and you're optimistic about other people. But for yourself, you're often pessimistic putting it under the guise of realism." A huge thing to think about.)
- I've learned who I think my real friends are and how much I love them.
- I've learned how it feels to have dreams come true. (amazing! great!)
- I've learned I can get what I want.
- I've learned how much I love/ need good office supplies.
- I've learned that I can have OCD tendencies (esp. about the house—a talisman against being alone, perhaps?)
- I've learned that I still don't know how to eat, how to build a consistent exercise relationship with my body—but I have hope about these things.
- I'm not good at relaxing.
- I don't like to be criticized or judged (unless I've asked for it or really, really trust the person talking to me.)
- I think I have a special destiny.
- I fear I have too many projects—but new ideas for me are the engine.
- I miss my family and friends.
- I'm not sure if I will have a baby.
- I am pretty disciplined and good with money (this can become OCD).
- I've learned that I can be cheap.
- I've learned that I will spend any amount on art. (Mariachis, hello!)
- I've learned that sometimes in another country you have to eat shit. (the girl at the party saying to me: "I saw that thing you did at Ex Teresa. I didn't like it.")
- I've learned to find humor in humility (see above).
- I've learned the power of cut flowers— their simplicity and beauty and cheerfulness.
- I've learned how things can turn on a dime, how each day can bring magic and surprise and banality and growth.
- I've learned how even the smallest things can find their way into art.

- I've learned how to trust myself more.
- I've learned that I have a bloodthirsty hate for mosquitoes.
- I've learned that I am emotionally reserved.
  This is more obvious to others than I realized.
- I've learned sometimes guys pick fights when they're scared that you don't have enough emotion for them and so they want to incite you to respond.
- I've learned that guys can be extremely emotional (Sexy/Mexy C.)
- I've learned what it feels like to really like a guy/
  miss him /want to be with him (E.).
- I've learned how good it feels to tell the truth
  and not care if you seem desperate (L.)
  —how this gives you power.
- I've learned that sex without condoms leads to U T I !
- I've learned that tattoos can be a mark of quiet, gentle shyness in a man.
- I've learned that in a year you can make a lot of casual friends and acquaintances in a place, get known in a scene—
  but that it would take much longer to really feel grounded.
- I've learned that some places offer an immediate spark—
  you know you want to be there.
- I've learned or at least am trying to learn not to take everything so personally.
- I've learned how to walk into a space and try to work.
- I've learned that I'm ambitious.
- If I were to go to Harlem or Paris now, I could do the work of the artist.
- I'm becoming a better artist.
- By doing it, you learn how.
- Emotional risk can lead to messiness, a sense of devastation, being hit by a bus, but can also take you to a brand new level as a person and an artist.
- Presentation ≠ Choreography ; Improvisation ≠ Experimentation
  -----> not automatically
- Keep your eye on the prize. No matter what!
- Poetry remains inextricable to my process, approach, art, life.
- I still have a hard time with the aftermath of a performance.
- Seeing others in passionate embraces can make me feel more lonely.
- This year has been hard, isolating, frustrating.
- This has been the best year of my adult life: what I've learned about myself, what I've learned about others, what I've done (in my body, in art, in the world).
- I am cracking (open) into bloom.
- I'm ready

# DEAR MARTIE

11/25/21

    Happy Thanksgiving! I woke up thinking of you as I often do, since your *Garden Kite* is right across from my bed. It makes me so happy to look at it in the mornings, to sip my tea and to think of you, powerful woman, making your own paper, working the pulp, drying and smoothing it, then sewing in red threads, floral fabrics, collaged images, mesh, and lace. It makes me think of a tricked-out kite, a wing at rest before breaking the frame and heading out again to flight.

    How are you, mujer? Did you share a holiday meal with friends or hang out on your own? I did something incredibly luxurious—politely declined two awesome dinner invitations to hang out in my pajamas and work all day on my Mexico book. Ooooh such bliss! Did I tell you about that? More than a decade since I first tried to circulate my Fulbright documentation, I finally have a chance to put it out there. But the timeline is bananas! Plus tracking everyone down has been kind of wild and catching up with people. It's hard to believe that so many folks who hung out with me every day have now completely disappeared! Or people I met and thought would be dear friends forever I never saw again. Well, really, you could say it was me who disappeared. Or lost touch. I haven't been to Mexico in so long that it breaks my heart. My Spanish has slipped. At least you and I are still connected.

    I thank my lucky stars that you were also a Fulbright Fellow that year, the most senior Fellow to boot. You had a quick smile but your eyes were discerning. "Gab," you said, "I'm in my 70s. I don't have time for things that aren't worth it. Hanging out with you! Now that's worth it," and then you laughed. And we would drink a beer or eat something good. Remember when I took you to my favorite seafood restaurant? I loved the soup and the grilled fish there and the green checkered tablecloths and the whole vibe. And you would tell me the best stories, about your first time in Mexico, studying with Siquieros and hanging out with the muralists and growing as an artist.

I've been doing studio visits with young artists at
CalArts and UCLA and remember what you told me. As one of
the first women admitted to the Pennsylvania Academy of Fine
Art, you must have been so proud to get in. But what you
talked about was how much you had to quit. "Gab, I didn't
like how they were training my eye to see," you said. And I
think so much about that. How are we training our eyes to
see? Or not see? What happens to the sight lines if we shift
to new places? Can we not only see new things but even see
in new ways? Or do we have to be in the right place to even
see something at all?

What did you see when you moved to Mexico? And then
when you moved from Mexico to Spain? I know like Elizabeth
Catlett, you felt "la flecha del amor." Love as a spur for
travel. I always marvel at how love can rescue us, astound
us, shift us—even though I'm such a tough cookie and
struggle to succumb like that. How do you know when to give
in, when to push back, and when to move on?

Martie, you're such a rebel! Even after leaving
Spain and taking a tenure-track job in the US, you quit the
academy again! I've been thinking about that too. How the
institutional structure wasn't right for you, the art you
were trying to make, the life you were trying to live. Even
though it's led to financial struggles, the loss of a steady
pension, you stand by your choices. I admire that so much,
Martie! You have to be tough to be glamorous, right?

237

Last time we talked, I asked, "Are you doing okay?" Right quick, you replied, "Don't worry about me, Gab. I'm a survivor!" You are my friend. Destiny's Child's got nothing on you! I want to live life more like that too. I'm still trying to figure out my place in the world, inside or outside the academy. I want to keep making art no matter what. Thank you for showing me one way to live. Hopefully, now that we can be triple vaxxed, I can finally come visit you in Roswell. It's been too long! I'm sending you so much love.

Muchísimos Besos,
Gabrielle

# DANCING ON ICE

Galantes, gitanas, gringos, chilangos, performanceras, tropicalizados, caribeños, y surtout les descendants de l'île d'hispaniola:

It gives me great pleasure to introduce "Bailando Sobre El Hielo" — comic stylings at the intersection of brainy black girl and post-Aztec New World warrior.

Ponce entered my world of performance art and now, as graphic, I enter his. Redrawn reality. Brown skin, white eyes and full lips at the global dawn of apocalypse.

*Ooh la la. Uh-oh.*

Was this intrepid black feminist performancera *ready for the world*? Ooooh Sheila!

To reckon with minstrel ghosts. To see *caricaturas* as potential exorcism. To open myself to la Fuzoo, global refractions of self through the prism of el Ponce.

Dancing on ice here is the drawn representation of our transformations "in and out of place"and the challenge, the thrill, the play of drawing representations themselves.

¡Àndale! Enough theorizing. Viva la fuzoo! Put on your dancing shoes!

-Gabrielle Civil
el 4 de julio (Independence Day, EEUU) de 2011

# Bailando Sobre El Hielo
## por Ponce + FUZOO

243

# DEAR PONCE

Wed, Apr 13, 2011 at 1:04 PM
subject: love+ comic+ race madness + opportunity!

Dear Ponce--
Please forgive the craziness of my recent correspondence.
It's so hard being away from people--not being able to speak
more directly or frequently. I love that you made this comic
in your own vibrant style and I love you! By no means, will
you need to do it all over. And yes still to using it and
having it be part of the documentation of my work in Mexico.

But let me explain why and how I wrote what I did before
and how I think it could work.

Welcome to Race Madness USA.

In one week, I was assaulted with extremely racist images.
On the cover of Vanity Fair magazine, there was a gathering
of "beautiful" stars and starlets--all white except for one
black man suggestively being stroked by a white woman and
one black woman--extremely light-skinned--wearing a tiger-
print dress and actually nursing a leopard cub in her arms.
That same week, I saw a movie where blacks were ridiculed
as being dumb and black women were called fat and ugly.
The same week, to try to unwind, I watched a popular show
in which the same extremely light-skinned woman passes for
white on the show and the only other black woman is fat,
black, and used exclusively for comic relief. In my class, I
am teaching a novel called "Push" (the basis for the movie
Preciosa")and so much of what she talks about is being fat,
black, ugly and either invisible or ridiculed. All of this
is telescoped in time, but is so much what I carry living in
this country. Here, I am fat, black and ugly. And this is
so much of what I tried to forget or escape or play with or
avoid or explain in my work in Mexico.

Everything is also amplified by my being back in MN right
now.

244

It is so white, so cold.
I am so invisible here.
So I came home after a long day, a long week, a long life
in this place and I was waiting for your attachments of
the comic to download and they were coming up at different
speeds. And the most amazing thing--the addition of color!
Black lines on white paper was so different than dark brown
skinned. It all became more loaded--
and artistically this is good.
The work is visceral, jangly, fuzoo!
But all of the mammy, sambo, racist images in the United
States of big lipped, big eyed black women are also in
color.

And when the first one downloaded was me in the yellow with
the squirrel and the tree and there she was--fat, black,
cheerful. I went crazy. Was she a mammy? Was she a
glamorous, black woman performance artist? Was she me? How
am I seen? Will I never escape? my own insecurities? years
of racist images that wear me down, erode my confidence and
creep up when I least expect it?

That's when I asked: "Is this how you see me? Am I this
unsexy?" And as soon as I sent it, I realized that I was
lashing out in a way that was so outside of you and that I
was tired and crazy but also that image, the image of me
with big lips and long monkey arms "salvaje y magnifica," me
making fun of Conrad, me being one of those women in Conrad,
those big shiny white eyes, it all was triggering a deep gut
level response. And that's when I wanted to step back and
think. Why was I responding this way? How do these images
relate to other images of black women in the US? in Mexico?
More rich thinking about being "In and Out of Place."
About my body, my life, my work . . .

So please forgive me again if I've caused stress or
confusion or made you feel like your work was unworthy. I'm
glad we're friends enough for me to be able to be vulnerable
with you and tell you about my feelings and to propose some
next steps.

It's important to have the comic in the world!
It can stay exactly the same.
Or if you want to reconsider/ talk with me
about the 3-4 specific images that make me nervous,

245

that's possible too. Either way, I'd like to add a short
meditation that goes with it that talks about what I just
told you and the struggle that I feel about representation.
What does it mean to have someone represent you?
What does it mean to see yourself in someone's eyes
--esp. if you are a proud black woman?!

I think the two things together--the comic and the
meditation-- would be super interesting and a cool
opportunity to put ideas, images, language in conversation.
They both would go in my catalogue--and also if possible,
in Replicante (my English translated into Spanish of
course.)What do you think?

And where are you now?
Have you already moved from the island?
Abrazos Primo--and my best to Dr. Andrea!
Gabrielle

# + RESPUESTA

from Rodrigo Betancourt
to Gabrielle Civil

Thu, Apr 14, 2011 at 4:47 PM
Re: love+ comic+ race madness + opportunity!

Prima,

No problem girl. Just right now I am stranded in an island
called ANTIGUA. A Soucuya, has cursed me ( I will let you
know the story when it's the right time) so it's taking a
lil bit to leave the West Indies.

Racism... ...girl I have learned so many things about life
in this 10 months in the Caribbean, that, to process all of
this it's going to take effort, and lots of imagination.

For me, the weirdest thing it's... When I see black people
treating black people with a different standard 'cause ones
they speak english and the others speak french. It's bad.
Andrea came back home a couple of times so disappointed of
the people from Dominica (doctors, nurses) cause simply they
just treat really bad the patients from Haiti or Dominican
Republic.

Cause I speak french or spanish am I supposed to stand this?
Am I a different category since I'm not like you?

And more... being in a lil Gringo Whitey Ghetto like is Ross
Campus, was the extreme.

Listening to things like:
THERE IS A MEXICAN TRYING TO BREAK IN YOUR HOUSE ANDREA...
Oh sorry it's your boyfriend!!!
or...
a white kid from Wisconsin shutting down Andrea's mouth
saying:
Oh no, 'cause after this, You are going to start to defend

Obama and We all here don't really like that Mr. President.
or...
THERE IS A MEXICAN BEHIND THE BAR!!!!

So, at the end, I totally understand you, and more, when I
see the stereotypes of latino people other cultures have
from us, or the worst, when mexicans claim themselves
they are mexicans cause they are not INDIOS cause the
worse insult in Mexico it's to be called PINCHE INDIO...
So disgusting all of this.... White light brown Mexicans
racists against brown mexicans with indigenous face, black
people english speakers treating like shit black people
french speakers....Black crackhead stealing and assaulting a
poor Kalinago old man who told me: I don't like to go to the
City, They are so tall and We are so short, that They always
abuse me....It's a mess.

I wrote in my memories after a breakdown: Kalinagos are
shades, British are ghosts and Dominicans are zombis...
cause, and this is how I feel this, its nobody's fault since
the people that created these standards, this view of the
world, are death long gone.

Imperialists slavers indian killers black people importers
are death and gone I hope in hell....The only thing for
sure, it's, to change this state of mind might take 500 more
years, and the solution does not look that easy...but, I
agree, I understand you, let's improve this comic.

World it's nuts.

Send me the list of images I will improve, so we make the
point about this issues, send me the page and the meditation
you have about all of this.

Amor espoir muerte y sacrificio.
I will be in Mexico next monday, give me an appointment
(time and date) to chat at least in chat in gmail or
facebook. Better would be to do Skype.

Abrazo muy fuerte.
Antigua West Indies.
--

PONCE+BTKS+FUZOO

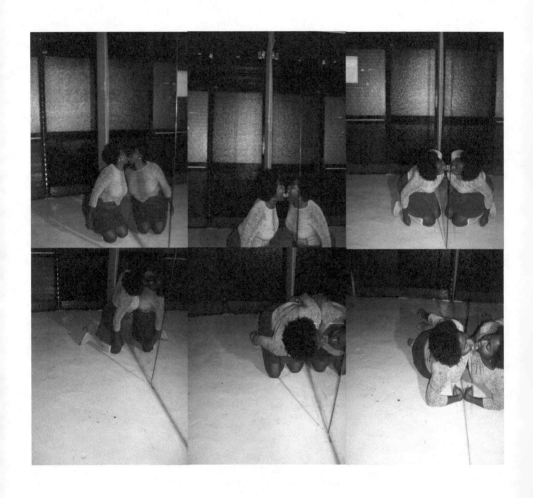

# MIRRORS

Rarely do I see reflections of myself in the world.
Caricatures, yes. Hattie McDaniel in a fat suit in *Gone With the Wind*. Tyler Perry in a dress. But a black feminist performance artist in a comic or movie or television show is still something unprecedented or unaligned with the narratives that always precede me. I'm not talking about Beyoncé. (Slay, Queen, with your films, with your entire media empire!) It might be different if I sang, but my work is something else, something more off the grid.

Certainly off the radar of Hollywood.

I'm not a sidekick or maid or Housewife on Bravo. I'm not comic relief, except for when it makes sense. If you can't tell by now, I take myself and my work very seriously. I like to create or enter environments and make something happen, with language, objects, feeling, sometimes other people, and always my dark, plump body.

When is someone like this the star of the show?

Or even shown at all?

Even or maybe especially living this life, I crave more and better representation. (One day, I'd like to change this Cassavetes-style aka feel free to send me donations to make my own movies.) In the meantime, it's a relief to meet other artists like myself to confirm that we exist.

Catron and I met through our mutual friends, Aleida and Jeza, two smart feminists from Oaxaca. While I was lucky to know some other black women in Mexico City, Margot, Alexis, Selena, and April, it was a thrill to meet another black feminist performance artist. Catron was pretty, smart, and funny. She had brown skin and short, curly black hair. She wore bright eye shadow and vibrant clothes. And she was passionate about Black Diasporic life in and across the Americas. Like me, she wanted to explore this life through performance.

While I come out of poetry, Catron holds a legit MFA in Acting from UCLA. She has done plays and mainstream work (*Days of Our Lives!*). She has lived in Los Angeles, the belly of the beast, and was put out by the limited visions of her there. Like me, she was called to the creative possibilities of somewhere else. It felt good to share our reflections.

When I say I could see myself in Catron, it's not to subsume her in me, but rather to revel in a mirror image. I wasn't singular and didn't need to feel that way. Patterns and prints splashed over chairs. Something to

251

hold onto forever—this memory—a happy swirling of music and cerveza. There were many of us there. Was it a farewell party? Was there a bag of clothes on the floor? Catron couldn't fit everything in her suitcase, so she was giving things away. We were dancing and laughing. We weren't saying good-bye. We could go our different ways and still stay in touch. She would come back and live in Mexico for years.

July 2, 2009
subject: destino

Marco!
So glad you got the message.
And I'm so excited again about your Fulbright.
From the start, I knew that you were meant to have it!
Hoooray!
You will be here when I'm supposed to be back over there,
but I really want to stay.
Maybe we can overlap??
Cheers,

Gab

* * *

Oct 28, 2009

Last night, when I was dropping off the laundry – I remembered visiting Purvi and Julia in NYC the year before I moved there. I would see people walking or with groceries or just look up and see people living in squares of light up in the sky. And I would think –

THEY LIVE HERE

and this last week, I've been very <u>internal</u>, very quiet, not going out much, not talking much to people, not taking calls, struggling with artistic process --->

And then those moments like last night when I walk out on the street and it's liquid dark and I chat about American politics in the laundromat and eat cheap, yummy tacos at the stand on Coahuila b/n Manzanillo and Insurgentes and pick up stuff at the pharmacy and walk over to the mall for guilty pleasure French fries and I realize something amazing

I LIVE HERE

I have a life in Mexico City that – even when I'm in "stand by" mode – affords such pleasure.

* * *

d e s p e d i d a

I don't need to have the grand gesture all worked out or know already everything that I want to say about <u>leaving</u>. But I want to show what it is I know or use this performance as a form of investigation.

there's something I need to work through
---> something about performance making farewell

Each piece this year has been a struggle. That's the truth.
Is there always in my process a moment of deep panic?
I know it didn't start this way
I want to believe this work has not been one of procrastination.
I want to believe in my <u>deep</u> principles, process, possibility -
instinct, gut, stamina – talent, intention, creativity, imagination
as an artist
I want to trust that those moments of internal turmoil, internal isolation
or just powdered doughnut, on-line TV are a weird kind of
REGENERATION

254

since I'm away from family, friends (deep chills), artistic comrades
since I don't have a lover right now
some deep reckoning with the self
an understanding of my own craving for people
– connected to my deep need for solitude


all of this has become a part of the work
performance    dealing with the flip side of glamour
saying goodbye


Friday Oct. 29, 2009
today is the day that it all has to come together.
This was my deadline and now I have to deliver
BELIEVING and DOUBTING

Right now, I'm fighting tension in my body – a headache, a mild
cough, that nagging pain in my left hip ---> I'm on my period (for which
I'm glad) – but my body feels more tender and I'm also operating on only
a few hours of sleep. The show is progressing, still more work to be done
– but I'm <u>doing</u> it – feeling and getting more grounded in it, feeling still
under the gun (the stress path to my hip is the testament) but feeling that
there is enough time, money, love (feeling momentarily crushed out by O.
doesn't hurt either).

Another good omen for magic – ran into I. and a friend of his on the
street. He recognized me immediately – and asked for me to send him info
about the show. He's someone I'd still like to be friends
with . . . Three weeks away from going home, still people I want to be
friends with. A bittersweet sign. For all my happy talk, I've been pretty
stressed out here the last couple months. There have been fun, good times
for sure but between the computer drama, money woes, artistic blocks,
Mexican bureaucracy, and romantic dead ends, it's been tough. Plus the
weather has been lousy and I haven't felt all that hot much of the time.

Madhu asked me how my spirit has been lately – and I think I've
been kind of down – but trying to rally.  Going to dance class when I can
(although I missed 2 weeks in October!) - keeping the house clean, keeping
up with work deadlines, swallowing some of my pride and running after
people who I feel should be running toward me.

Madhu asked me today how I felt about leaving Mexico – and this
is a key part of the piece – how do I really feel about leaving Mexico City?

disconnected  hiding out      biding time
resigned       relieved        incredulous
emotionally    shut down       internal
disbelieving      sad          uncertain about
wondrous       unsure          the future (in general
wondering      stressed out    + my future in this place)
      kind of wanting ---> one last hurrah!


\* \* \*


despedida!
a black woman wears white
a black woman is a white dove
a black woman is tied to the land
           to a chair
     daydreaming and wandering

In Mexico, I've faced a lot of my fears
---> and it feels like there are more possibilities
how much if any of this will actually go into this piece?
     How much do I want to reveal
     of my feelings of farewell to the audience?
If this isn't the revelation – what is <---
     my body in space
the opportunity for images and actions


\* \* \*


     She's leaving home
     will you say it to me
     That word < adios.
     It's not enough
     I need you to trace it
         on my skin
     tracery of the body on paper.

# DESPIDIDA

a performance work by Gabrielle Civil

Date:        November 5, 2009

Venue:       Galería Interferencial, Mexico City, Mexico
             1a Cerrada de 5 de mayo No. 14 PH,
             Centro Histórico, México DF CP 06000
             (Metro Zocalo)
             Entrada Libre


Concept:              — my farewell to Mexico —
                      most important element => tracery
             a tracery—offering, a description of what has been here
             a leaving with a trace in the gallery space
             a leaving with traces of experience
             on my body, on my dress, in the air, on my skin
                      sub-element => a going away party


Influences /Inspiration: simplicity: the idea of Lorena Wolffer's
performance in China & Francis Taylor's Mexico performance at
el Chopo; the dove flying away in the holy spirit prayer card I got
in Veracruz; Laura Sutherland describing body tracing in her art
therapy class and her emotional breakthrough sharing her work to her
classmates; Aravind saying in that difficult moment "I miss the text"—
and the impetus to reveal, share, return to the original Gabrielle Civil
performance contribution—alternative circulation of poetry in space.


+w r i t i n g    o n    t h e    b o d y

<u>Tone / Aspirations</u>:
I want to create something beautiful, simple, (well relatively simple since simplicity is not so much my performance paradigm), clear, strong elements / gestures—but with some layering; a tone of connection, interaction, fun but also something a little haunted or sad—a good-bye—I want the piece to feel embodied, warm—this is not exactly "after this, you will love me"—but maybe a little "love me now, because after this, I'm gone. . . ." maybe with a little wistfulness, relative spareness, wry humor, absurdity, black woman body, white, paper, cloth, grace in this piece, I am saying farewell to Mexico + Mexico—embodied by the audience—is also saying farewell to me—we both have to have an encounter for this farewell to be meaningful—traces of this encounter have to be left/ felt on both sides.

# despedida

performance art by Gabrielle Civil
with Catron Booker & Daniel Hernandez

## invocation

DANIEL and CATRON arrive each with a bottle of tequila.

They set these down by the altar and pick up their texts from the altar.

They stand for a minute and breathe. They look out and see

GABRIELLE arrive in a red dress and a big black sombrero.

In her arms she has a large roll of paper.

She unrolls the paper on a diagonal line in the space.

She takes a step and says *tracery Mexicana*.

DANIEL starts to read. CATRON starts to read.

Gabrielle makes her way to the altar by tracing first her feet

and then other parts of her body on the white paper.

When she arrives, she writes the word "despedida" on the wall

and then traces her hand over the word.

She moves to the altar, hugs DANIEL, hugs CATRON

and picks up her text.

DANIEL and CATRON move to the white wall.

*despedida* INVOCATION

Catron

AGOSTO

SEPTIEMBRE

OCTUBRE

NOVIEMBRE

DICIEMBRE

ENERO

FEBRERO

MARZO

ABRIL

MAYO

JUNIO

JULIO

AGOSTO

SEPTIEMBRE

OCTUBRE

NOVIEMBRE

Daniel

ARRIVAL

HUELLA

PIÑATA

RASTRO

VESTIGIO

PIZCA

MAGIA

NEGRA

CUERPO

DULCE

DOLOR

DESEO

DELEITE

DESPEDIDA

TRAZA

aquí estamos
a key in a lock
a click. a turn.
arrival
his torso
un masaje
mentiras
a map wet in the rain
errors
errante
getting lost
learning streets
getting to work
here come the whites!
mis ojos mis dientes
¡Viva México, cabrones!
I am the magic negro
en el mercado
en viva la música de
salsa
las velas en la pastel
variations in time
nunca apprendí
las manganitas
nunca dejé de pensar
para accionar
pero intenté
in the parque mexico
me enojo contigo
pain with each step
los dulces abajo
de mis pies
huelitas
obama & mlk
me enojo contigo
my sister
we traced turkeys
with our hands
dias de gracias
cerillos, cepillos
BRUSH
back home snow
Rosa
Acapulco
Ira
les baguettes

mariachis
mlk & obama
in and out of place
say it loud
candy shoe
mi tío
ex voto
una pérdida
una paloma
Minneapolis
tie air
aftermath
¿dónde está
la comida de la calle?
yoga
the sea
mi cuerpo
las chakras
the second one the most
my mother
my father
la falta del agua
lilies for easter
historias de la muerte
contagio
influenza
los puercos
fantasmas
ghosts in the street
isolation chamber
grinding away
delays
delights
cuerpo, lenguaje, espacio
muño
tlaxcala
yo tengo una pregunta
tonta
que hacemos aquí
dolor mata dolor
his tattoos
in and out of place
viva tatuajes
viva struggle fall

caída de pétalos
amarillos
mi otro vestido rojo
home again
abrazos
lazos
ligas
regreso
problemas
de compu
imagen concepto acción
tie air Puerto Rico
cortaron mi pelo
sacrificio de
performance
they cut my hair
madhu
my phone is death
eléna and russell
problemas de
respiración
conexiones falsos
dos círculos centrados
trágate el pez
swallow the fish
michelle
veracruz calor
bailando en las calles
internal quiet
alone lograre?
solita desplome
where the hell
is the plumber?
purvi
frio y dudas
variaciones de
electricidad
una marcha de
electricistas
suspenso suspensión
despedida
where we are now
pronto pronto me voy
pero no sin trago, no sin
una traza - not without
with a trace

# mexico tracery

GABRIELLE reads a poetic account that traces her time in Mexico.

DANIEL and CATRON trace each other on the wall as she speaks.

## instructions

*No quiero irme sin rastro, sin traza. I refuse to leave without a trace,*
*Entonces, vamos a hacer una cosa. Catron, Daniel, ¿dónde está el papel?*

CATRON and DANIEL stop tracing on the wall and go and get the paper.

GABRIELLE, CATRON, and DANIEL spread paper on the floor.

GABRIELLE gets the markers from the altar, spreads out on the paper on the floor.

GABRIELLE gives the instructions. the equivalent of:
"Uds. tienen que trazarme. Yo necesito una traza de mi cuerpo de cada uno.
Van a trazarme. Van a estar trazado. Van a trazar los otros aquí.
Aquí están las paredes, aquí está el papel, aquí está mi cuerpo.
Vámanos. Empezamos."

## body tracery

The music starts. CATRON and DANIEL help the crowd start the tracery.
DANIEL begins tracing me. Catron starts tracing someone else.

Three songs play: "She's Leaving Home,"-Syreeta, "A Milli"-Lil Wayne and
"So Long Farewell" from *The Sound of Music*.

At the end of the last song CATRON and DANIEL get up and move the
people back beyond the line of the white paper on the floor. CATRON and
DANIEL then go and get their bottles of tequila.

GABRIELLE gets up, looks at the space, and gets her bottle of tequila from
the center of the altar.

## cantina chorus

GABRIELLE says: "I think we need a drink. Es una despedida, verdad, vamos a echar un trago traza de espíritus, línea liquida en el cuerpo. Hemos trabajado. Vale . . ." Antes de llegar a México, mi idea de México era amigos felices cantando en una cantina. Canciones cursis y legendarias. Aquí están copas, vamos a tomar un poquito . . . Y también, cantamos . . . Cantad todos gente—por favor—es mi despedida, dame este favor vamos a tomar, a cantar, a bailar—solo para una canción más! Lista . . .

DANIEL, CATRON, and GABRIELLE pour tequila and distribute limes. Once the crowd is ready, the music begins.

"O Cielito Lindo" plays. People, sing, dance, drink . . .

GABRIELLE makes her way back on to the paper in the center and, at the end of the song, prepares for the next action.

## adios

Gabrielle pulls out a black marker, pulls down her dress, and starts to write *Adios* all over her body. This takes time.

## final leaving

Gabrielle puts the marker on the altar, blows a kiss to the crowd and leaves. **Somehow the party needs to keep on—Erick can put on music—hay mas chelas! y mas tequila . . . vamos a festejarnos un poquito más!** or something . . .

## stairwell trace
On her way out the door, Gabrielle leaves something in the stairwell for the public to encounter later.

# Despedida en galería PH
## por Sergio Peña

Todos reciben plumones de colores y dibujan, siguiendo los contornos del cuerpo de la artista recostada sobre un piso cubierto de papel; luego, motivados por la artista, todos se dibujan entre sí o a sí mismos, siguiendo los contornos de sus cuerpos, brazos y piernas recargados en las paredes cubiertas de papel del recinto. Todos aprendieron pronto a representarse, todos participan. Y es evidente que no es sólo ella la que "deja huella"; se deja una huella colectiva enorme, diversa, según el tamaño de la persona o su intensidad... Dejar huella, es de lo que se trata. No haber pasado de largo, por ejemplo, un año viviendo en un lugar. Y si no bastara con esa acción gráfica colectiva para haber conseguido algo, se escucha de pronto la voz de la artista intercalándose con las voces de otros colaboradores: palabras en inglés, español, inglés, español, *espanglish*, *Engloñol*, de pronto ahí está todo, en ese discurso que todo lo abarca y todo lo comprende, un año de vida mexicana con equipaje norteamericano que se entremezclan a tal grado que constituyen una identidad propia, nueva, rica.

De pronto un brindis colectivo en vasos tequileros con una porción simbólica de tequila para cada uno de los asistentes y de fondo una canción de *The Sound of Music: Adieu, Good-bye!* y la artista desaparece y la huella que deja es tan fuerte que el público aplaude como esperando un *encore*. Pero no ocurre, la artista no vuelve a aparecer, mientras en la habitación todos aguardamos por largos minutos y experimentamos emoción, nostalgia, alegría, una dulce sensación de pérdida, la misma que se llega a sentir cuando se deja el país al que se ama. Y entiendo de golpe que ella se salió con la suya...

Eso sólo puede ser arte, no hay otra explicación.

Le stoy las gracias al Espíritu Santo por la oportunidad de vivir y hacer el arte del Performance en México por 15 meses. Y a ti Santísimo Espíritu Santo dediqué mi último Performance en este país y este se llamó: "DESPEDIDA". te ruego me permitas volver a este maravilloso país. Gabrielle Civil
México, D.F. 5 - noviembre 2009.

# Farewell at PH Gallery

## by Sergio Peña

## Translated by Lucía Abolafia Cobo

Everyone gets a marker and draws an outline of the artist's body as she lies down on the paper-covered floor. Then, motivated by the artist, everyone delineates each other or their own body, arms and legs outlined as they lean against the paper-covered walls of the room. Soon, everyone learned to represent themselves. Everyone participated. Moreover, it was evident that not only was she "leaving a print" but that there was a huge, diverse collective imprint, according to the size or intensity of each person...

It's about leaving an imprint. For example, having lived in a place for a year without letting it go by. As if it weren't enough getting something with such a collective graphic action, the voice of the artist can be suddenly heard as it alternates with the voice of other collaborators—words in English, Spanish, English, Spanish, Spanglish, Engloñol—and suddenly everything is there, in a speech that covers everything and understands anything, a year of a Mexican life with American baggage intertwining to such a degree that it constitutes a new, rich and owned identity.

Suddenly, a collective toast with a symbolic serving of tequila in shot glasses for each and every member of the audience is raised. In the background, a song from *The Sound of Music*: "Adieu, Good-Bye!" is playing as the artist disappears. The imprint left behind is so strong that the audience claps as if waiting for an encore. But it doesn't happen, the artist does not show up again. Everyone waits in the room for long minutes as we experience emotion, nostalgia, joy and a sweet sensation of loss—the same one that is felt when leaving the country that you love. Then, I suddenly understand that she has gotten away with it...

And that can only be art. There is no other explanation.

In memory of Elizabeth Catlett, who blazed the trail of black women's art in Mexico.

In memory of Audre Lorde, who went to Mexico and blessed us with biomythography.

In memory of bell hooks, incomparable visionary
who innovated black feminist thinking, writing, and living.

&

In memory of Martie Zelt, my dear friend who chose life as an artist until the very end

*Ashe*

# Production History & Notes

"Here Come the Whites," (1.5 min), EJECT 2, Segundo Festival Internacional de la Ciudad de México, juried exhibition, Ex Teresa Arte Actual Museum, October 2008.

"Me Enojo Contigo," Parque Mexico, Mexico City, DF, November 2008. A mirror installation of this work was exhibited in "Irreversibles: Contemporary Women Artists," curated by la Niña Yhared & Beatriz Rebollar at Casa de Yhared, Mexico City, November 2009 .

"BRUSH," Pasagüero, Mexico City, Mexico City, DF, December 2008, reprised at Obsidian Arts Gallery in Pillsbury House, Minneapolis, MN, April 2010.

"In and Out of Place (MLK & Obama)," Paseo de la Reforma, Mexico City, DF, January 2009.

"Tie Air" (after my experience in La Congelada de Uva's *taller de performance*), Center for Independent Artists, Minneapolis, MN, March 2009.

"Muño (*fantasía de la negrita*)" Performagia Encuentro Internacional de Performance, Museo del Arte de Tlaxcala, Tlaxcala, Mexico, June 2009, reprised at Obsidian Arts Gallery in Pillsbury House, Minneapolis, MN, April 2010. The text of this performance appeared in the 2009 Performagia catalogue (ed. by Pancho López) and my chapbook of performance writing ( *ghost gestures* ), published by Gold Line Press at the University of Southern California in 2021.

"In & Out of Place (México, DF)," Museo Ex Teresa Arte Actual, Mexico City DF, June 2009.

"despedida," Galería Interferencial, Mexico City, DF, November 2009, reprised at Obsidian Gallery in Pillsbury House, Minneapolis, MN, May 2010; Catron Booker and Daniel Hernandez contributed opening gestures in Mexico City; Michael Abdou and Rosamond S. King did so in Minneapolis.

In & Out of Place *ex votos* made with Gustavo Villeda appeared in the solo exhibit "In & Out of Place," at the Obsidian Gallery, Minneapolis, MN, May 2010 and in the LatinFest group show at the California Institute of the Arts, March 2019.

My Fulbright project "In and Out of Place" generated other works including "<<MN <->MX>>", a short video that premiered in the online festival Low Lives 2, in April 2010 and then was featured in "TRAMPOLIM," Galeria Homero Massena, Vitoria, Brazil, Jan. 2011 and Low Lives @The Vault, SPACES gallery, Cleveland, OH, 2013, all curated by Jorge Rojas.

The excerpt from my critical essay "In & Out of Place," and the critical responses by Sergio Peña, Selena La'Chelle Collazo, Daniel Hernandez, Juma B. Essie, and Pancho López, with translations by Lucía Abolafia Cobo were all part of an In & Out of Place monograph started in 2010 that ended up not happening, or rather is happening now. These writers had been audience members for the performances and were commissioned to write their reflections. Many thanks to St. Catherine University for initially supporting this work.

"Obama, Mariachis & Me" was published in "the Expatriate Issue" of Inside Mexico, Feb. 2009.

"Flashbacks" was published as "Inicio from In & Out of Place" in Gulf Coast: A Journal of Literature and Fine Arts, Volume 35: 2, Spring 2023.

Bailando Sobre Hielo by Rodrigo Betancourt (Ponce) was published in Revista Replicante in July 2011.

Color fields throughout this book were inspired by Fox Whitney's online Color Swatch Catalog for his 2020 Melted Riot show at the Henry Gallery in Seattle. The states of being of the color fields double later as covers for two of my studio notebooks, lovingly transcribed by River Hollows.

# Image Credits & Permissions

Quotation from Elizabeth Catlett Mora from "The Negro People and American Art" in *Freedomways*, Issue 1, Spring 1961. Public domain. Spanish translation by Gabrielle Civil.

Quotation from Frida Kahlo found in *Frida* by Hayden Herrera. Copyright © 1983 by Hayden Herrera. Used by permission of Harper Collins Publishers.

Quotation from Ralph Lemon comprises 2 sentences from *Geography: Art/ race / exile* © 2000 by Ralph Lemon. Published by Wesleyan University Press. Used by permission.

Quotation from Guillermo Gómez Peña from "In Defense of Performance Art" in both English and Spanish from the artist's website. Used by permission.

Spanish translations of Kahlo and Lemon by Lucía Abolafia Cobo with permission. Catlett epigraph translated by Gabrielle Civil from the public domain.

All images, artworks, and photos in this book used by permission.

Cover photo and photos of Gabrielle in red ball gown at El Ángel & El Ángel in blue sky by Camilo Hannibal Smith.

Photos of Gabrielle and la Congelada de Uva by Tania Gomezdaza.

Photos from *Muño (fantasía de la negrita)* by Pancho López.

Photos from *In & Out of Place (México, DF)* by Edith Medina except for the photos of the audience taking pictures of Gabrielle (in "Devil Dance"), the photo of Ponce (with "Ponce Pirata") and the photo of yellow rose petals falling on Gabrielle in the ¡Viva! finale by Pancho López.

Photos from *despedida* by Rodrigo Jardón Galeana including the photo of Gabrielle in a sombrero (with "An Intervention").

*Bailando Sobre Hielo* comic by Rodrigo Betancourt Ponce.

Ex votos paintings by Gabrielle Civil & Gustavo Villeda.

All other photos, video stills, and artbook images by Gabrielle Civil / courtesy of artist.

# Libros

Zami-Audre Lorde
*Filles de Mexico*-Sami Tchak
*Geography*-Ralph Lemon
*Art on My Mind*- bell hooks
*A Long Way from St. Louie*-Colleen J. McElroy
*Escape to Berlin*-Adrian Piper
*Aurora Americana*-Myronn Hardy
*A Rock, A River, A Street*-Steffani Jemison
*An African in Greenland*-Tété-Michel Kpomassie
*Wandering*-Sarah Jane Cervanek
*Mémoire Errante*-Jan J. Dominique
*Wandering Memory*-Jan J. Dominique (trans. Emma Donovan Page)
*Meeting Faith: The Forest Journals of a Black Buddhist Nun*-Faith Adiele
*Elizabeth Catlett: An American Artist in Mexico*-Melanie Anne Herzog
*The Diary of Frida Kahlo: An Intimate Self Portrait*
*The Repetition of Exceptional Weeks*-Rajnesh Chakrapani
*Exercises for Rebel Artists*-Guillermo Gómez-Peña & Roberto Sifuentes
*Performance y Teatralidad*- Josefina Alzácar
*Down and Delirious in Mexico City:The Aztec Metropolis
in the Twenty-First Century*-Daniel Hernandez
*Geopoetics in Practice*-ed. Eric Magrane, Linda Russo,
Sarah De Leeuw, and Craig Santos Perez
"The Flame Through the Bridge"- by Antena Aire (Jen/Eleana Hofer + JDPluecker)
*African by Legacy, Mexican by Birth*-Marco Villalobos & Ayanna V. Jackson
*Afro-Mexico, Dancing Between Myth and Reality*-Anita González
*Arte No Es Vida: Actions by Artists of the Americas,
1960-2000*-ed. Claudia Calirman, Elvis Fuentes,
Ana Longoni, Robert Neustadt, Robert & Gabriela Rangela
*Reversible Monuments:Contemporary Mexican Poetry*
-ed. Mónica de la Torre & Michael Wiegers/
*The African Presence in Mexico: From Yanga to the Present*-Sagrario Cruz-Carretero
"Experimentos en Alegría: un libro de ejercicios"
-compiled by Gabrielle Civil (trans. Jumko Ogata Aguilar)

# *In & Out of Place*

# Agradecimientos

A flotilla of people were involved in the development of *In & Out of Place* over the last decade. This includes my *cuates, galanes y chambelanes* in Mexico, my Minnesota peeps, my OG squad, my Detroit family, my Antioch people, my Cali crew, and more. Below is my appreciation to loved ones who have long offered me support as well as my best attempt to remember everyone from the original Fulbright performances through the multiple iterations of this book. My apologies to anyone whose name has been lost in the intervening years. Please know that I appreciate you from the bottom of my heart. <3

Always thanks to God, the ancestors and my family, Kate Frances Civil, André Civil, Yolaine Civil, Herman Kern, David E. Smith, Jr., Walter and Myrtle Jean Jones, Kathy Jones, Walter Eric Jones & their kin.

Special thanks to River Hollows for their transcriptions of my notebooks. Deep thanks to other folks who worked on earlier iterations of this project: Anna Ruhland, Molly Davy, and Jessica Ashley Nelson (2011-2012); Jane Foreman (2016) and the indispensable Hannah Priscilla Craig (2019-2021). It took a while, but this work has finally come to light!

Thanks to Edith Medina, Mónica Mayer, Victor Lerma, Lorena Wolffer, Rocío Boliver (La Congelada de Uva), Juan Carlos Juarena Ross, Elizabeth Catlett, Gustavo Villeda, Marco Villalobos, Daffodil Altan, Daniel Hernandez, Juma B. Essie, Pancho López, Sergio Peña, Rodrigo Betancourt Ponce, Selena La'Chelle Collazo, Lucía Abolafia Cobo, Mariachis México Internacional, Jennifer Josten, George Flaherty, Wendy Vogt, Anita Khashu, Nicole Guidotti Hernandez, Martie Zelt, Margot Lee Shetterly, Miré Regulus, Mankwe Ndosi, Josina Manu Maltzman, Ellen Marie Hinchcliffe, Sarah Stockholm, Laura Milkins, Therika Mayoral, Rodrigo Jardón Galeana, Iván Farias Carillo, Jonathan Farias Carillo, La Niña Yhared, Beatriz Rebollo, Gina Dabrowski, Aravind Enrique Adyanthaya, Ana Manatou, Erick Diego, Catron Booker, Aleida Lujan Pinelo, Jezabel Lujan Pinelo, Sául López Velarde, Madhu H. Kaza, Rosamond S. King (esp. for the long talk about the Fulbright in the Casablanca airport), Purvi Shah, Zetta Elliott, Eléna Rivera, Russell Switzer, Moe Lionel, Dennie Eagleson, Laura Sutherland (your quarantine apartment was a lifesaver), Donald Harrison, Michael Abdou, Greg Bullard, Eric Leigh, Jeremy Braddock, Ira Dworkin, Rafael Cervantes, Allison Adrian, Amy Hamlin, Tia-Simone Gardner, Jorge Rojas, April Anderson, Caroline McKinnon, Oliver Avedaño, Cleila Cifuentes Gomez Pezuela, Camilo Hannibal Smith, and my amazing danza contemporanea teacher Victor Vizcarra.

Thanks to the administrators and curators of the US Fulbright Commission & the J. William Fulbright Scholar's Program, COMEXUS (Comisión México-Estados Unidos) & the Fulbright García-Robles fellowship, Museo Ex Teresa Arte Actual, Museo Universitario del Chopo, and Galería Interferencial in Mexico City; Center for Independent Artists, Minneapolis, MN, Museo de Arte de Tlaxcala in Tlaxcala, Mexico; Casa Cruz de la Luna in San Germán, Puerto Rico (where I also showed *Tie Air*); Saint Catherine University, St. Paul MN, especially the Departments of English, Women's Studies & Critical Studies of Race & Ethnicity, the Faculty Resource Center, and the Academic Community Development Committee for early support of this project. Thanks to the California Institute of the Arts for steady employment and the good vibes of LatinFest. Thanks to the UCLA Art department for the cherry on top.

Thanks to Tisa Bryant, Janet Sarbanes, Ken Ehrlich, Jess Arndt and Litia Perta, Anthony McCann, Michael Leong and Cacao Díaz, Nicolas Daily (Black Power Think Tank), Sarah Williams and MJ Balvanera at Feminist Center for Creative Work, Sharon Bridgforth, Omi Osun Joni L. Jones and the Diaspora Project for West Coast support.

Thanks to my Writing Group (WG) Andrea Quaid and Allison Yasukawa for keeping sacred writing time. Special thanks to Allison for helping me think through the essay about black women and travel and questions of cross-cultural desire. Thanks also to Lewis Wallace and Catherine Edgerton for writing with me across the interwebs. Special thanks to Rachel Moritz, for thoughtful reading of this manuscript and the reminder to trust my intuition.

Extra special thanks to Julia Saénz Lorduy for smart, sensitive reading and for encouraging me to trust my readers and myself.

Thanks to Katie Jean Shinkle for inviting this work into the Innovative Prose Series and to J. Bruce Fuller, Peter "PJ" Carlisle, Karisma (Charlie) Tobin, and the Texas Review Press team.

Thanks to Faith Adiele, Chloë Bass, Selena La'Chelle Collazo, Ph.D., Carribean Fragoza, and Pancho López for the kind blurbs.

Special thanks to Mexico for offering new challenges and inspiration.
You will always have a place in my heart.

"[P]erformance art . . . is neither acting nor spoken word poetry. . . . We theorize about art, politics and culture . . . We chronicle our times [and] our accounts are non-narrative and polyvocal . . . . [O]ur main artworks are our bodies, ridden with semiotic, political, ethnographic, cartographic and mythical implications. . . . We are what others aren't, say what others don't, and occupy cultural spaces that are often overlooked and dismissed."

"El arte del performance... no es interpretar ni hacer poesía escénica. . . . Teorizamos sobre arte, política y cultura. . . . Confeccionamos la crónica de nuestro tiempo (y) nuestras maneras de contar no son narrativas y sí plurilingües. . . . Nuestras principales obras de arte residen en nuestros cuerpos, conquistados por todo tipo de implicaciones semióticas, políticas, etnográficas, cartográficas y mitológicas. . . . Somos lo que otros no son, decimos lo que otros no dicen, y ocupamos espacios culturales que a menudo son obviados y rechazados".

—Guillermo Gómez-Peña

# Out